Solving Life:
Mastering Decision Making with Investment Wisdom

Pavlin Kumchev

Solving Life:
Mastering Decision Making with Investment Wisdom

Copyright 2025 © Goodle Publishing

This is the sole work of the author, and no portion of this publication may be copied or re-published in any publication without express permission of the publisher or author.

Edited by Chris Murray and George Verongos

ISBN: 978-1-0369-1676-3

Disclaimer

The views, thoughts, and opinions expressed in this book belong solely to me, Pavlin Kumchev, and not necessarily to my employer, organisation, committee, or other group or individual. While I currently hold the position of Managing Director at a global multi-strategy hedge fund, this book is the result of my personal journey and experiences. It is written and published as an independent work.

The information provided in this book is for general informational and educational purposes only. None of the content constitutes professional financial advice, nor does it represent the opinions of any financial institution or business with which I am affiliated. Readers should consult with a professional advisor or conduct their own due diligence before making any financial decisions based on the material in this book.

While real-life experiences, anecdotes, and narratives form the basis of discussions herein, some details and characteristics have been altered to protect the privacy of the individuals involved. Any resemblance to actual persons, living or dead, or actual events is purely coincidental.

I have made every attempt to ensure the reliability and accuracy of the information provided in this book. However, the information is provided 'as is' without warranty of any kind. I do not accept any responsibility or liability for the accuracy, content, completeness, legality, or reliability of the information contained in this book.

Neither the publisher nor the author shall be liable for any losses, injuries, or damages from the display or use of this information or from any actions taken based on its contents.

For M. and A.

I love you dearly.

Contents

Preface 1
Introduction: The Most Beautiful Woman, Monte Carlo,
and My Boys 5

Section 1: Organised Randomness

Chapter 1: Understanding Randomness:
Monkeys and Miracles 17
Chapter 2: Mastering Risk: Turning Variability
into Opportunity 29
Chapter 3: Fallibility of the Average: Embracing Variability 43
Chapter 4: Avoid the Snake Eyes 53
Chapter 5: Bells and Fat Tails 61

Section 2: Cheap Options

Chapter 6: Chess, Backgammon, and Poker 85
Chapter 7: Value Investing: The Hunt for Cheap Options 97
Chapter 8: Cheap Options in Life 119
Chapter 9: Contrarian Investing 129
Chapter 10: The Psychology of Cheap Options 137
Chapter 11: Plan A, Plan B, and Daredevils 143
Chapter 12: Trade-offs and Sacrifice: Solving Life Backwards ... 151
Chapter 13: Candy Crushing and Hidden Sacrifices 163

Section 3: Embracing Life's Cycles

Chapter 14: The Value of Suffering 169
Chapter 15: Cycles: Always Make Big Circles 177

Epilogue: Life With No Regrets 191
Acknowledgements 197

Preface

What if the principles that guide the world's most successful investors could also illuminate your path through life? This book began as a deeply personal endeavour—an attempt to distil the lessons I've learned over decades into something meaningful for my sons. Dear M. and A., my love for you is unwavering and relentless, and this book is dedicated to you. But as I reflected on my journey—growing up behind the Iron Curtain, forging a career on Wall Street, and navigating life's peaks and valleys—I realised these lessons hold immense value for anyone striving to make better decisions, overcome challenges, and live without regrets.

For more than twenty years, I've been immersed in the fast-paced world of global finance. My career catapulted me to the world's top financial and investment institutions, including Morgan Stanley, Blackstone, Carlyle, and a premier global investment hedge fund, where I learnt the art and science of investing and business analysis from the best in the world. I have steered investments across six continents and witnessed the delicate interplay of risk, reward, and resilience. My career has taught me a profound truth: success—whether in finance or life—isn't just about luck or talent. It's about preparation, perspective, and the courage to act when it matters most.

Yet the most transformative role of my life hasn't been in the boardroom but at home. Fatherhood has shown me that true fulfilment comes not from personal achievements but from passing wisdom to others. My sons have been my greatest teachers, reminding me that knowledge, just like love, only thrives when shared. This book, inspired by countless conversations with them, is my attempt to offer you the same guidance—to equip you with the tools to navigate life's uncertainties and unlock your potential.

Life, like investing, is unpredictable. It's shaped by randomness, chance, and the decisions we make under uncertainty. Both have finite timelines, and both demand careful stewardship of resources—whether it's money, time, or energy. Over the years, I've seen great risks yield staggering rewards, careful strategies unravel in the face of bad luck, and seemingly small choices compound into life-changing outcomes.

This book isn't about financial advice. It's about something far more valuable: a framework for making better decisions in the face of life's complexities. We'll explore a set of principles from the world of investing—focusing on randomness, risk, probability distribution and optionality—and use them to improve the way we navigate uncertainty towards a more intentional life. If you are looking for stock tips or high-octane stories from the world of finance, you're in the wrong place. If you're looking for a sharper lens through which to view even mundane, everyday decisions, welcome. Drawing from the principles of value investing, the psychology of risk, everyday examples, and lessons learned through both success and failure, this book provides a roadmap to help you build resilience, seize opportunities, and live a life you would choose to relive.

My own story begins in a small country behind the Iron Curtain, where I was born under a communist regime that shaped much of my childhood. I've queued for bread during economic collapse when the regime failed and negotiated high-stakes deals in corporate offices across the world after immigrating West as a teenager. I've travelled to more than 50 countries, lived on four continents, worked with and befriended people from all walks of life—experiencing both the harsh constraints of chance and the boundless possibilities of choice.

These contrasts shaped my philosophy: while we can't control where life begins or sometimes even how it immediately unfolds, we hold immense power over where it ultimately takes us. The principles that guided me through financial markets—managing risks, leveraging opportunities, and embracing uncertainty—are the same principles that can help us overcome adversity and thrive.

The book is structured into three sections. First, we'll explore chance, randomness, and risk—those unseen forces that shape our lives. Next, I'll share actionable strategies for making better decisions in life rooted in value investing and show you how to identify opportunities—which I call 'Cheap Options'—with high upside and minimal downside. Finally, we'll reflect on life's broader cycles, exploring how to find meaning in life's challenges, adapt to the inevitable changes we all face, and make the deliberate sacrifices that will lead us to our dreams.

At its core, this book is about hope—not the passive kind that waits for fortune to intervene, but the active kind, built through preparation and persistence. Life will test you, and sometimes failure can dim the courage and ambition of youth. It is in the unwavering determination to push through the challenges and inevitable setbacks—recognising they are necessary stepping stones to success—that hope lies and where there is wisdom to be found. Life will present both challenges and opportunities. My goal is to equip you with the tools to navigate these moments so you can build a life not just of success but of purpose and fulfilment.

The same principles that guide great investors can guide us all—because life, like markets, is full of uncertainty, volatility, and opportunity. This book gives you a framework—not advice—for making better choices when it matters most. Let's begin.

Introduction: The Most Beautiful Woman, Monte Carlo, and My Boys

What if the best framework for living a good life wasn't found in philosophy or psychology but in investing? What if you could take the mental models of the world's leading investors and use them not just to build wealth but to build wisdom? Have you ever considered whether you could approach life as if it were an equation to be solved for the best possible answer? Or, as an investment you are looking to get the greatest return on? Imagine applying the same decision-making principles from investing to navigate life's complexities and uncertainties. This book aims to show you how.

In *The Matrix*, Neo, played by Keanu Reeves, senses something 'off' about his life and the world around him, driving him to seek answers. He discovers that the world he knows is a simulated reality called the Matrix, created to control and subdue humanity. This resonates with many of us. We often feel like we've surrendered control, reacting to pre-existing commitments, responsibilities and societal expectations. Chance also plays a crucial role—one we often underestimate. Some of the most important events and the deepest emotions in our lives—love or jealousy—fall outside our control, much like how unpredictable market forces influence investments.

Great success and catastrophic failures often stem from the same forces of chance, acting in opposite directions. While our birth is a random event entirely outside our control, our unique starting points—abilities and socio-economic status—play a vital role in how our lives unfold. In finance, experts refer to this as *path dependence*: the sequence of events leading up to the present influences the value of an investment and the investment decisions we make. History is important in determining potential outcomes. If you generate exceptional returns on seven investments and then lose money on the next three in your portfolio of ten, your fund is likely to still do well. However, if you start your investment mandate with three losses, you may never get to number four if investors in your fund lose faith and pull out their money. Whether you are born rich or poor, with a high or low IQ, your skin colour, gender, religion, and place of birth all determine how your life could play out. Unfortunately, all these characteristics fall entirely outside our control.

Life is much like a boxing match: a blend of reacting, defending, and seizing opportunities amidst the randomness of each punch. We have limited and precious time before the final bell of the bout rings. We spend a big part of the fight reacting and defending to survive. We take a few premeditated shots, but also need a lot of luck to land a good one, and we get a few unlucky ones on our chin as well. About a third of the match (let's call it eight hours of sleep), we are spread out on the floor, knocked out or recovering. It feels like we are on autopilot. A series of automated reactions often shapes our lives, and like characters in *The Shawshank Redemption* movie, we can become institutionalised by the very walls and constraints we once despised. As Morgan Freeman's character, Red, poignantly states, 'First you hate 'em, then you get used to them. Enough time passes, it gets so you depend on 'em. That's institutionalised'.

This book aims to create a system of rules—a decision-making process—that leads to optimal outcomes, taking back control of your life, and setting you free. While I can't define your life's purpose or what would make your journey worth it, we can agree that the optimal outcome is a life you would look back on with no regrets. Here is a way to judge your life, analogous to a metaphor the Nobel-prize-winning author Milan Kundera proposes about true love. Imagine when you die, you knock on the doors of Heaven. God asks you, 'Do you want to go back, be born again, and live the exact same life you just did, not remembering this conversation, or would you prefer to try a different life'? If you choose to relive your life unchanged,

Introduction: The Most Beautiful Woman, Monte Carlo, and My Boys

you've lived well. The goal is to live in such a way that you would choose to relive your life, with all its decisions and outcomes, without regret.

In my 20 years in the finance industry, focusing on investing, I have dedicated my professional life (most of my conscious life) to the art and science of predicting the future and making optimal decisions, recognising that you never have a crystal ball. My career has taught me to analyse risks, measure performance, and distinguish between luck and skill. The principles of making superior investment decisions apply not just to finance but to everyday life decisions and long-term goals. This book explores key investing and risk management lessons, culminating in a decision-making strategy optimal for both investing and life.

My career has also taught me to focus on one fundamental question: 'How do I maximise value'? This question is central to both investing and living. Maximising the value of our lives means ensuring no regrets when looking back at the end. Value isn't just monetary; it's about achieving our personal best and fulfilling our dreams, whatever those may be. Like a well-performing stock, life's successes are measured by how close they come to realising our full potential, given our unique circumstances at the time.

Searching for a Decision-Making Framework

Decision-making in life and investing share many parallels. Both involve making choices with imperfect information in a complex environment influenced by randomness and risk. Like an investment, life has a beginning and an end, with a limited number of days and years. Our starting points and the myriad variables around us shape our paths. Can we solve this life equation and make an investment with the best possible outcome?

Imagine parallel universes where your life unfolds differently in each of them, based on a combination of your choices and random events. In some instances, the path is long. In others, it is short. In some, you achieve great success and happiness. In others, you face failures and regrets. Of course, a great many, if not most, of these paths are likely to be similar. As we established, your life's path depends highly on your starting point. *However, the gap between the best and worst possible outcomes is vast.* How do we ensure we get the best one?

I began seeking a decision-making framework early in my career, influenced by a 2008 article titled 'Case Closed for Free Will?'. It described a study showing that our brains often make decisions before we are consciously aware of them. This raised the unsettling possibility that our choices might be predetermined. The study, conducted by Dylan Haynes and his team of researchers, found patterns of brain activity that could predict people's decisions up to ten seconds before they became aware of them. Fourteen subjects lay in a functional magnetic resonance imaging (fMRI) scanner, instructed to decide spontaneously whether to press a button on the right or left. They could take as much time as they wanted to press the button but had to report the moment of their conscious choice. Remarkably, researchers could see brain activity patterns predicting their choices well before the subjects consciously made them. This discovery suggested that our minds make decisions before we are even aware of them, raising the question, 'Is free will an illusion'?

Determined to take control of my own life, I designed a rigid decision-making framework that, regardless of whether a subconscious algorithm was at work, would allow me to steer my life in a chosen direction, even if I could not control my immediate reactions. It was a system of preset rules for every scenario. If someone betrays you, move on and leave them behind. If a friend needs help, always be there, no matter the time, place, or cost. However, this system was too inflexible, black and white, and doomed from the start. We let ourselves down so often, whether it's a plan to eat more healthily or drink less or the infamous New Year's resolution to hit the gym three times a week. How could I expect others to never disappoint me if I would sometimes disappoint myself? The system was not flexible enough to accommodate the subtle nuances of life and the plasticity required to navigate its complexity. Over time, my investment intuition and hindsight lessons from risk

Introduction: The Most Beautiful Woman, Monte Carlo, and My Boys

management refined my approach and provided the foundation for a more effective framework. It is this framework, I call 'Cheap Options', that is at the heart of this book.

The Statistics of Better Choices

When I look back, my introduction to two groundbreaking statistical models helped me realise just how influential statistics could be in guiding major life's decisions: the first is a statistical optimisation process known as *the most beautiful woman* problem; the second, a predictive model called Monte Carlo simulation.

The Most Beautiful Woman Problem[1]. The most beautiful woman problem (also known as the optimal stopping problem) has fascinated me for years. It's a statistical dilemma that seeks to determine the best choice from a set of candidates based on a sequence of observations. Imagine you are tasked with selecting the most beautiful woman from a group of 100. You cannot see them all at once but only observe each woman once in a random sequence, unable to return to a choice you have previously dismissed. This problem highlights the trade-off between choosing too early and potentially missing out on a better option later, or waiting too long and settling for a less desirable choice. When is it optimal to stop and make your decision?

One strategy offers the maximum probability of success. At the start, you simply observe and dismiss a fixed number of candidates to establish a baseline for comparison. Then, you choose the first option better than any previous one. How many candidates do you purposefully dismiss at the start to establish this baseline? According to this strategy, the answer is: 37 per

---

[1] This author's distinct wish is to avoid offending anyone with this formulation. Since the 1950s, this problem has been presented with different names, including references to beautiful women, male suitors, secretaries, and others. They are each a product of their time, and you should feel free to replace both the words beautiful and woman with different ones of your liking. This is simply the name I stumbled upon for the algorithm, which captivated me as an adolescent.

cent of all. Applying this method of choosing the best candidate offers the highest probability, which is elegantly the same as the proportion of candidates you dismiss: 37 per cent.

I vividly remember my Eureka moment when I encountered this optimisation problem and its neat solution. The 37 per cent rule struck me as both profound and practical. It provides a relatively high probability of success while allowing for ample exploration. Equally, you are spared the disappointment of exploring a lot more options (whatever these may represent in life), only to discover the most desirable one was left behind. The best option could be patiently waiting for you at number 99 or even 100. It's just that 37 per cent is the highest probability ever reached, progressively declining as you move past the 37 per cent baseline.

You may wonder: 'Can I use this strategy in my private life? Should I stop dating and settle down at that exact point'? But what is 37, and does it have to be out of 100? Think of 100 as a percentage you can apply to any number, be it 20, 10, or perhaps romantically, only 1. 'Try everything, retain what is good', as the Bible advises. Well, maybe try just 37 per cent of everything in this case!

Optimal stopping theory can help you decide when to commit to any choice, maximising your chances of making the best one. In their book *Algorithms to Live By*, authors Brian Christian and Tom Griffiths explore many applications of the strategy, from the optimal age to get married to which house to buy or rent. The algorithm naturally simplifies the complexities of real-life scenarios. Allowing candidates the right to decline (for example, in the context of a marriage proposal) lowers the probability of success. In contrast, the ability to revert to an option previously dismissed or having prior information on the candidates raises the rate of success to more than 50 per cent.

Introduction: The Most Beautiful Woman, Monte Carlo, and My Boys

Regardless of how practical the strategy truly is, the most beautiful woman dilemma first ignited my curiosity about applying statistics and probability management to optimise decision-making in real life.

The Monte Carlo Simulation. A Monte Carlo simulation is a powerful statistical tool used in finance to explore the range of potential outcomes influenced by a number of variables. Each variable has its own range of potential values, some more probable than others. In these simulations, we explore different possible futures by running hundreds of thousands of 'what if' scenarios, incorporating the full gamut of potential outcomes for each variable.

Given the vast number of scenarios, the simulation often creates a bell-shaped curve of all potential outcomes, each a dot but together resembling a continuous line (see the illustrative chart below—we will explore this curve and its significance in greater detail later in the book). The most likely outcomes (occurring most frequently) are clustered in the curve's middle section, representing the results' central tendency. The best (highest value) outcomes appear at the right-hand side tip of the curve and are possible but less probable. Similarly, the worst (lowest) outcomes are to the far left but are also less likely. While most outcomes are similar and clustered in the middle section, the gap between the best (far right) and the worst (far left) outcomes is vast.

11

When I started my career in finance at Morgan Stanley in New York, advising on deals in the healthcare sector, the Monte Carlo simulation was just getting introduced within the firm as a novel tool for scenario analysis. It was a departure from the standard analysis of the usual three scenarios when looking to predict the performance of a business and its valuation: *base case* (the most likely outcome), *downside*, and *upside* scenarios. I volunteered to join the cross-team task force, looking to trial the tool on real projects and create a case for its broader roll-out across the firm. Since then, whenever I reflect on how to solve for the best outcomes in life, I think of the curve above and how to push outcomes all the way to the right.

Remember our parallel universes, each unfolding based on different choices and random events? Your life in most of these universes may be similar, as they all have the same starting point. However, some may diverge substantially due to chance and poor or, conversely, great choices you make. The possibilities are endless. But your life here, in this universe, is only one. The goal of this book is to create strategies that push your outcome toward the exceptional right-hand side tip of the curve.

My Boys: The Inspiration for This Book
Conceived initially as fatherly advice to guide them through life's complexities, this book was born from love for my two sons. They have taught me that the greatest miracle in life is life itself. Recognising that I couldn't shield them from all the mistakes they might make, my aim was not to prevent the errors of youth but to equip them with the tools to avoid repeating mine. Drawing from my extensive experience in investing, probability, and risk management, I sought to teach them how to make better decisions and reach farther than I have. Progress stems from the ability to rely on the wisdom and experiences of others as stepping stones to new and higher dreams.

Our journey began with simple lessons, such as how not to fall from a tree branch (or, more precisely, why not to climb it). From simple games of

Introduction: The Most Beautiful Woman, Monte Carlo, and My Boys

dice and coin tosses, it evolved into strategic games like chess and backgammon, each offering valuable insights into risk and decision-making. These games served as practical metaphors for life and incorporated strategies also used in investing, illustrating the nuances of risk and reward.

Friday mornings, when I usually drive my sons to school, became our classroom. Eventually, to capture these teachings more efficiently, and perhaps to their relief, I began recording our conversations. Later, I transcribed them and refined my thoughts on my laptop instead of in front of my 'students', leaving more time for fun in the 'classroom'.

I felt fully immersed in our discussions and saw profound lessons for life in simple rolls of the dice or tosses of the coin, illustrating the role of chance and the power of perseverance. I am drawn by the beauty and wisdom in the simplest things. I feel like that boy Douglas Spaulding in Bradbury's *Dandelion Wine*, bidding farewell to his best friend who is leaving Green Town to spend the summer with his father. Douglas finds himself wandering through familiar streets in his idyllic town after the bitter-sweet goodbye until his eyes are suddenly drawn to the beautiful stained-glass windows of the local church. The boy has never paid attention to them before. He becomes aware of the overlooked beauty around him, all the wonders hidden in plain sight, the undiscovered treasures woven into the texture of everyday life.

This book draws on all the lessons I have learned from investing to find such treasures full of lessons that can be applied to life. It's about creating a decision-making strategy that helps us live our best lives, making choices that lead to the optimal outcome, just as we aim to make the best investments.

Section 1
Organised Randomness

You are in the driver's seat of your car, confident and in control. But statistically, the person on a plane, anxiously surrendering control to the pilot, is far safer per mile travelled. Why do we trust ourselves more than the numbers? This surprising contrast between perceived and actual safety highlights an important truth about life: our sense of control is often an illusion, and our instincts can lead us astray.

In this section, we explore the elusive nature of randomness and probability, which intricately shapes our existence and decisions. We'll explore why the outcome with the highest probability may not always be the one that actually happens, shedding light on the fallibility of averages. Understanding this concept is crucial as it reveals the significance of tail risks: those rare but pivotal 'snake eyes' events that can turn our world upside down. We also introduce Six Sigma events, extremely rare occurrences that remind us that what seems improbable can profoundly impact our lives or help us navigate a journey of continuous self-improvement.

Building on these insights, this section paves the way for the 'Cheap Options' strategy, a key proposition of this book detailed in the next section and a powerful tool for optimal decision-making based on value-maximising investing principles.

Join me through the following chapters as we explore the invisible forces of randomness and risk that shape every decision we make. These concepts may seem abstract, but they are the bedrock of strategic thinking. By the end of this section, you'll have a solid grasp of these forces, setting you up to leverage them in the next section, where we apply these insights to real-world decisions. Together, we'll discover how embracing uncertainty can lead not just to survival but to a thriving existence in a world governed by chance.

Chapter 1
Understanding Randomness: Monkeys and Miracles

What if your greatest outcomes in life had less to do with your talent and effort—and more to do with coin flips you never saw? We like to believe we're in control. But the truth is, randomness—pure, unfiltered luck—plays a starring role in who we become. Let's confront that uncomfortable reality.

While skill and merit matter, life is shaped by randomness and chance. I would make an even bolder suggestion: the defining forces and events in our lives are often outside our conscious control. We don't consciously decide who to fall in love with; the verb 'fall' itself is imbued with weightlessness and loss of control. We don't decide what our children may be like, their characters, struggles, successes, and how those impact us in return.

The death of someone we love and the torment and anger it stirs within us. The colour of our skin, our sexual preferences, the place we were born, and the time. Did we feel love and nurturing care when growing up, or did we witness violence? Are we born poor or rich, and what school do we attend? What is our IQ? What is the level of serotonin in our blood, or the clinical deficiency of it, sinking us into permanent and intolerable depression? Are we born to a devout Christian family somewhere in the Midwest United States or to a devoted Muslim family in a small village in Pakistan? Would you be denied a place in Heaven if your God is not the true one by the chance event of where you were born?

Luck Is All Around

What we are speaking about is commonly called 'luck'. Good luck is randomness that works in your favour. Bad luck is randomness that works against you. Luck is a powerful influence on the outcomes and successes or failures of our lives.

Individuals often underestimate the role of chance, both in their successes and failures, when, in reality, unpredictable and uncontrollable factors play an overwhelming part. I remember a time when a seemingly random event drastically changed the course of my life. It was a chance meeting with an old acquaintance at a coffee shop. We hadn't seen each other in years, but that conversation led to a business opportunity I never anticipated.

Few areas illustrate the importance of luck, or the lack thereof, better than investing. Throughout my career, I have seen an equal number of brilliant minds who have never reached the peak of their potential and due recognition, as I have mediocre professionals who got catapulted to stardom by hitting a lucky streak or just being at the right place at the right time.

Luck is a fickle friend, but having it early in life is better than having it late.

Getting lucky at the start can build a reputation and provide you access to resources (including the ideas of others) that may be hard to defeat, even for a powerful enemy, such as subsequent bad luck. In life, as well as in investing, early impressions matter. Having luck in the beginning can make a world of difference.

Here's a scenario that illustrates the potential for luck to change outcomes and success. Imagine, for a moment, a world where investors could only bet on the red or blue fighter in a boxing bout, instead of betting on stocks and bonds. Both fighters are about the same size and height, made of pure muscle and determination. They are each capable of inflicting extraordinary damage and knocking the other one out. Investors in this fictional marketplace must choose red or blue as the winner in each round. Once the round is over, the fighters and the respective odds change.

After each round, you decide to randomly place your money (or that of those who have entrusted you with their life savings) on one of the fighters before each round. Like betting on red or black at the roulette table, without appreciation for the boxers' respective skills and odds of winning, you spin the wheel, close your eyes, and hope for the best. Each round, the chance of you being right, without doing any work whatsoever or having any skill, is 1 out of 2 or 50 per cent.

A simple statistical calculation would show that the probability of getting all the calls right, entirely by chance, 12 rounds in a row, is 1 in 4,096. This may look like a relatively small probability, but consider that there are more than 30,000 hedge funds globally, as suggested in a 2023 *Financial Times* article and based on information by data provider Prequin. Assuming they each have five to ten investors working for them, this results in anywhere between 150,000 and 250,000 professional investors. This means that around 40 to 70 investors can be expected to guess the correct result 12 times in a row, entirely by chance.

Now, imagine red or blue is the entire stock market or a specific stock going up or down in any given month, and the rounds are the 12 months in a year or 12 years in a row. You can make a seven- or eight-digit income that year in a large hedge fund on sheer luck alone. And suppose you recognised, albeit begrudgingly, that your success was due to chance more than to superior investing skills or flair for the sport of boxing. Knowing that luck has an expiration date, you may be tempted to make an even larger bet next round, predicated on hope and chance alone, more than fundamental analysis. Remember that you most likely get a percentage of the winnings, so a larger bet and greater risk promise a greater return.

Indeed, some would run out of luck quickly. Still, others may go on for several rounds, amassing an excellent reputation for skilful selection. Such reputation translates into great personal wealth, helping them raise large sums of money and receive fees in return for their investment 'skill'. Until their luck finally runs out or they are wise enough to quit.

At a lecture he gave at the University of Florida's School of Business, the great Warren Buffet asked a group of MBA students to imagine the following social system based on a barrel with roughly 5.8 billion balls, the world's population at the time. Within this new world order, representing a random system, each ball would determine important factors such as birthplace, IQ level, gender, ethnicity, skills, and parents. 'If you could put your ball back, and they took out at random 100 balls—and you had to pick one of those, would you put your ball back in'? he asked. The catch is that you wouldn't know which ball you'll get the next time around. As of 1998, 5 of those 100 balls, Buffet advised, will be American. 'So, if you want to be in this country, you'll only have 5 balls [to choose from]', Buffett explained. 'Half of them will be women and half men... Half of them will be below average in intelligence and half above average in intelligence'.

He asked the students again: 'Do you want to put your ball in there'? With the reasonable assumption that all those young MBA students in the room, men and women, were above-average intelligence, the imaginary lottery had already played out. 'Most of you will not want to put your ball back to get 100', continues Buffet. 'So, what you are saying is: [each of you is] in the luckiest 1 per cent of the world right now sitting in this room'. Buffet's message was clear: each student in real life had won life's lottery. But he took the argument further: a desirable social system would be one where you would live a good and dignified life, regardless of which ball you picked. This would be a system where the significance of randomness and sheer luck would be replaced by rules that allow for a desirable outcome, regardless of chance.

Such a system is the ambition of this book: to help define rules that allow for a desirable outcome regardless of chance.

Anything Is Possible... Statistically!

How does one go about living a life that is not completely subject to chance? Begin by changing your mindset about the power of randomness. You have more control over luck than you might think.

But this raises a crucial question: are we active agents in our own lives or merely spectators of events we cannot control? I think the answer is the same as the answer to the following: 'Would you rather be left amidst the tempestuous sea of chance in a ship with a rudder and sails or on a raft, carried in all directions at the whim of the sea'? This book won't help you predict the sea, but it can help you build a ship you can successfully control and steer as you navigate life.

The first glimmer of hope that we can somehow have some control over randomness is the knowledge that, statistically, anything is possible. Desirable outcomes can emerge from sheer randomness, and as the book later reveals, such outcomes can be pursued systematically with an increased probability of success. In his book, *Fooled by Randomness*, Nassim Taleb dives into the profound impact of randomness on our lives. He uses an amusing metaphor: a troop of monkeys, each hunched over a typewriter. If a sufficiently large number of monkeys were given typewriters and infinite time, one could eventually reproduce Homer's 'Iliad' word-for-word entirely by chance. Consider a simpler example: if a story starts with the word 'once' (as in 'once upon a time'), and the monkeys randomly type four consecutive letters, there would be 26 possible choices for each letter. This results in 26x26x26x26 or approximately 457,000 four-letter word combinations (most nonsensical, of course). The probability of spelling 'once' correctly, though entirely by chance, would be 1 in 457,000. Typing out the 'Iliad' word-for-word is statistically highly improbable but not impossible. A masterpiece is born out of total randomness.

The vastness of time and possibilities renders even the most unlikely events plausible. The creation of our planet Earth and Darwin's theory of evolution are two prime examples. Earth formed 4.5 billion years ago from a complex sequence of countless astrophysical events. These could have branched out at every given step into an almost infinite set of possibilities as particles collided and dust and gas accreted into larger masses. At the time of its formation, the chance of Earth evolving into what it is today, 4.5 billion years later, would have been astronomically small, yet here we are. A vast period of time, combined with a practically limitless number of possible outcomes in an endless universe, resulted in the miracle of Earth (for those of you more scientifically minded).

Consider the observable universe: with a radius of about 46.5 billion light-years (one light-year is around 9.7 trillion kilometres), its vastness is hard to grasp. Imagine scaling Earth down to the size of a virus. In comparison, the observable universe would roughly measure the size of our solar system! Take this vast space (fill it up with monkeys and typewriters in your mind, if you will), and add the tens of millions of years over which Earth is believed to have evolved. It becomes clear that our planet's existence today is a product of endless possibilities. Is our world a work of art written by monkeys?

Allow for enough time and space with infinite variations, and anything is possible, even if not probable. Unfortunately, our life spans are less than a blink of the galactic eye. Not much happens at all, relatively speaking, in the 80 years we have (if we are lucky) within the space limits of the town where we were born (only about 30 per cent of the global population lives outside their place of birth) compared to 4.5 billion years and the entire universe of possibilities.

Follow my rough maths here: take away, say, seven-eight hours of sleep, an hour to take a shower, brush teeth, get dressed, two hours of daily commute to work (I hope yours is less than mine), and we are left with a tad more than 40 years at best for work, family and everything else. Factor in eight hours (10 to 12 or even more if you will) of work, and you are left with

Understanding Randomness: Monkeys and Miracles

no more than 10 years for your family and any other passions you may wish to pursue.

And if your family is your passion, here is something motivating for you: you will likely spend most of the time you will ever spend with your kids by the time they are 10 years old. We are out of time from the moment we are born! We get one big chance in life, at best two or three. Some get none. We don't have the luxury of wasting time and opportunities. We need real skill, as monkeys are in short supply. *We need a strategy for life that maximises what we can achieve.*

At the extreme end, the perfected pinnacle of this approach is what I call a miracle. A miracle is an improbable event that occurs in a materially shorter timeframe than you would otherwise expect if it were entirely due to chance (Earth's creation in six days would be a miracle). I believe that we, individually and as a society, can achieve such rare outcomes. And if you are convinced that Earth and all living creatures were created by God as opposed to a prolonged and gradual process, this book won't try to prove you wrong. It will merely observe that you believe in miracles.

Guiding Forces Behind Randomness: From Miracles to Rules

While everything is statistically possible, and even miracles can happen, the lesson in this book is not to rely on miracles. Instead, it focuses on creating a system that increases the likelihood of such rare, seemingly miraculous outcomes—or at least makes them more probable. One example of this can be found in the miracle of life on Earth.

Consider Darwin's explanation for life on our planet. His *Theory of Evolution* suggests that randomness and chance play a pivotal role in the diversity of life. Mutations—random changes in an organism's DNA— provide the foundation for natural selection. Chance events like natural disasters (think meteorites) or climate and geographic shifts can determine which individuals survive and thrive. Yet, within this framework of randomness, natural selection acts as a non-random process, favouring traits that enhance survival and reproduction. Randomness allows for a range of possibilities from which the most advantageous traits are selected. So, even though chance plays a part, there is a guiding force that works to shape more adaptable and resilient outcomes over time. A guiding force within a sea of randomness.

Taming randomness with the power of a calculated guiding force is common in both life and business. Imagine a bustling business idea incubator, a hub where a flood of ideas, some brilliant, others half-baked, pour in from all directions. The goal is to ultimately arrive at winning business propositions with powerful potential. This scene mirrors the unpredictability of life itself, filled with random chances and chaotic twists. But here's where it gets interesting: despite the randomness, a clear, rule-based structure is the backbone of this incubator. It systematically sifts through the chaos to generate desired outcomes. High-risk ideas without commensurate high return potential, or those with flawed fundamentals, are rigorously vetted and ultimately discarded. What emerges from this disciplined funnel are the few robust ideas ready to soar. This is much like crafting a rule-based strategy for life's decisions.

Consider a weather metaphor—a must for any Londoner. Say you want to collect rainwater for your garden. In August 2022, Thames Water, the UK's largest water company, implemented a hosepipe ban due to extreme weather conditions and some of the highest temperatures on record. Rain, like many life events, is unpredictable. Yet, successfully collecting rain is possible with the right structure in place. If you put out a bucket and wait patiently, you're likely to catch some, eventually. You can't control when it will rain, but you can control your readiness to benefit when it does, ensuring your bucket fills up sooner or later.

Having a structure in place is critical, and following its rules and prescribed steps correctly is paramount to success. Think about cooking a stir-fry: you start with the vegetables that take longer to cook, like carrots or broccoli, and add quicker-cooking ingredients, like spinach or peppers, later.

If you change the process and reverse the order, you'll end up with a dish that's both overcooked and undercooked, disappointing your dinner guests. The same principle applies to decision-making in life and business: follow the right steps in the right order, and you'll achieve the desired results.

We can steer life's randomness toward favourable and often predictable outcomes by implementing a structured decision-making process. This method doesn't remove life's unpredictability—it masters it, turning wild chances into calculated successes.

Randomness or chaos is indeed the norm rather than the exception, and individuals and societies try to establish rules and systems of organisation that seek to limit the chaos and establish predictability and control. They build ships with rudders, strong masts, sails for direction, and heavy anchors so the boat can stand still and strong and persevere when it needs to. It is challenging to plan and make complex decisions in constant flux. Societal and political structures and hierarchies, including democracy, communism, or capitalism, have well-defined rules and values.

From the moment we wake up and tidy our beds, we introduce order and structure into our lives. As we grow up and learn to manage and direct our own lives, we start to help introduce order in the lives of others, our friends, children, or colleagues. We can then go further to empower, structure, and reduce the chaos in our communities, broader society, and why not the whole world? Moving away from randomness and reliance on luck into rules-based decision-making is the only way to improve outcomes in both investing and life. We must collectively change our frame of reference and recognise that who we are today is not immutable and predetermined but largely due to chance. Focus needs to shift from what we *observe* today as just one of the potential manifestations of endless possible scenarios to the *rules and process* of making efficient choices and achieving desirable future outcomes.

Let's revisit two scenarios from this chapter to show you what I mean. The first is the chance meeting I had with a friend that led to an amazing career opportunity. The meeting was lucky, but the follow-up was deliberate. I was prepared to take the opportunity that was offered. When randomness opens the door, be prepared to walk through it.

The second scenario involves our red and blue boxers. I described how pure luck alone can drive exceptional outcomes … for a tiny minority of investors. However, remember that the odds of blue or red winning changed after each round as the different boxers faced each other in the ring. This means that each round allowed the alert investor to do more work and improve the odds of winning by betting on the more experienced fighter. With rigorous analysis of the boxers in each round, not to mention analysis of their past fights and unique techniques, you could consistently pick winners with a probability of success well above a 50/50 chance, equivalent to a coin toss.

By the time you reach the last chapter, I hope you start thinking about every achievement or failure in your life not as a discreet, immutable outcome but as one that has played out from myriads of possibilities—possibilities that you have the power to influence. Such a mental framework is vital to making better decisions in life and investing.

In this chapter, I have set the stage for five important themes I want you to keep in mind as you read along:

- o You can optimise your probability of success by deploying a decision-making strategy from the world of investing, which I call the 'Cheap Options' strategy. It reduces the risk of being irreversibly knocked out of the game while preserving your chances for success. This decision framework requires you to understand the risks and rewards involved in making any choice. Don't get hit.

- Similar to investing, you need to take contrarian views, hold your conviction, and not give up in the face of adversity to outperform relative to others.
- The importance of sacrifice against a set goal. The greater the goal, the greater the sacrifice required. 'Solve' your life backwards from the stated goal.
- Life, nature, and financial markets alike move in cycles—the lows and the highs of those cycles are inextricably related and engender one another. The seeds of hope hide in the deepest desperation. Life does not move in a straight line, and you should not plan as if it did.
- You can control and actively manage the circumstances of your environment to engineer desired outcomes. Don't forget that happiness is relative, and compare it to where you started, not to where others are.

Before we go in-depth into these topics, however, we must get to a common understanding of what risk is and how to visualise the set of potential outcomes. Understanding the connection between skill, luck, and expected outcome is also essential. As you read along, I will refrain from getting into discussions that are too technical and difficult to comprehend without specialised knowledge in a given area. My approach and writing style aim to make the book enjoyable, approachable, and valuable to anyone who may pick it up. It is a dialogue. You can agree or disagree with me, and I will often give you the opportunity for the latter. By the end of it, I hope you have a few theoretical frameworks to make better choices or, at the very least, a few interesting examples and stories to share at the dinner table.

Recall a moment when life surprised you with an unexpected event. Did you see it as a challenge or an opportunity? How might your life have changed if you had embraced it as a stepping stone to something greater? Consider the biggest factors in your life—where you were born, the family you were raised in, the people you've met—how many of them were truly within your control?

Have you ever taken full credit for a success that might have been influenced by luck? If randomness plays such a powerful role in shaping outcomes, how can you position yourself to benefit from it rather than be its victim?

Key Takeaways: Chance shapes our lives profoundly, often when we least expect it. But we don't have to drift aimlessly on a sea of uncertainty, letting it dictate our direction. By recognising the role of luck, we can better prepare ourselves to seize opportunities and minimise risks when the unexpected happens. Randomness may be unavoidable, but with the right strategies, we can tilt the odds in our favour. The key is not to resist chance but to harness it—turning uncertainty into an advantage rather than an obstacle.

As we've seen, chance plays a decisive role in shaping our lives. But how do we deal with the uncertainty it brings? In the next chapter, we'll explore how understanding and managing risk can provide us with tools to navigate this randomness more effectively, ensuring that we are not just at the mercy of chance but can steer our decisions toward success.

Chapter 2
Mastering Risk:
Turning Variability into Opportunity

Randomness can create unexpected opportunities, but it also introduces risks. Both positive and negative outcomes are part of the journey, and how we manage these determines our success. This chapter explores how understanding risk empowers us to make better decisions, even in the face of uncertainty.

You've probably heard the stereotype that Italian men are irresistible lovers, smooth and charming when enticing their desired partner. Throw in images of red Ferraris, fine wine, luxurious fashion, and sun-soaked Mediterranean scenery, and the fantasy practically writes itself.

Now, I don't want to alienate any Italian readers or deny them their due, but let's poke a hole in that myth. There is a story of an Italian man who is asked about his reputation as an irresistible seducer. His response reveals a far more mundane approach: he spends his nights at the piazza, asking every woman he finds desirable to go out with him. Eventually, one of them says, 'Yes'. It isn't magic. He's not a master seducer; he's playing a game of probabilities. Like a savvy investor, he's managing downside, embracing rejection, and maximising opportunity. In some ways, it's the same game you play each time you swipe 'right' on your dating app.

This chapter delves into somewhat less romantic games involving dice and coins to illustrate basic concepts of chance and probability—methods I use to teach my kids the fundamentals of risk. Whether we realise it or not, understanding risk is key to navigating life's uncertainties.

Probability and Variability

Imagine you have a 100-sided die, numbered 1 to 100. If you roll it, the probability of getting any particular number—let's say 5—is 1 out of 100 or exactly 1 per cent. The chance of rolling a 1 is the same as rolling a 5, 50 or 100. Each outcome here is equally probable. Probability measures how likely an event is to occur. If you are rolling a regular six-sided die instead, the probability of hitting a particular side jumps to 1 in 6 or around 17 per cent. And with a two-sided coin flip, the probability of getting heads or tails rises to 50 per cent or 1 in every 2.

In life, just like with dice, things rarely turn out exactly as we expect. Let's say you are baking several cakes using the same products and recipe. Even though you follow the steps perfectly each time, no two cakes will ever taste exactly the same. Or picture skiing down the same slope a hundred times—each run will leave a slightly different trail, even though you favour certain routes more than others. This variation is called 'variability'—the greater the range of possibilities, the greater the variability we experience relative to the outcome we expect.

When you roll a 100-sided die, there are 99 other numbers besides the one you hope for. With a coin flip, there is only one other possibility. Variability tells us how wide the range of possible outcomes is, while probability shows how likely each one is to happen. Now, imagine investing $1,000 in the stock market, which has returned 10 per cent on average each year over the past five years. You may expect to generate a 10 per cent return or $100 this year as well, based on that average. But stock market returns are notoriously volatile, marked by wide variability. You could end up making far more than the 10 per cent return you expect, or you could lose much of your investment. This brings us to risk.

Two-Sided Risk

Risk is the uncertainty that comes with variability. Think of your 7 a.m. appointment on a freezing winter morning, relying on public transport. You risk being late and missing your time slot if there are delays or arriving too early and shivering outside. The probability of landing at your destination exactly at 7:00 is slim. Risk is the gap between what we expect and what could and does actually happen.

In investing and life, the word 'risk' tends to carry a negative connotation. We don't worry about the 'risk' of winning the lottery. Risk is usually associated with a chance of loss or failure. It represents negative outcomes relative to expectations—taking a slight turn from your usual ski path down the slope and hitting rocks. But here's the key: variability doesn't only bring threats—it also brings opportunity. The downside of risk might be losing half of your investment, but the upside could be gaining 50 per cent. Understanding risk is all about recognising both sides of the coin. Think of it this way: when you expect to make a 10 per cent return but get 15 per cent instead, the 5 per cent incremental gain is your upside. Any return well below 10 per cent or a loss is a downside. In investing, the worst risk is losing your principal—the initial amount you put in. Nothing stings and damages your reputation more than losing part or all of your initial investment.

In sum, every decision carries inherent variability, and the degree to which the actual outcome differs from our expectations defines our experience of risk. In investing, this is seen as the spread between expected returns and actual results. In life, it's the difference between our plans and reality.

While risk usually has a negative connotation, I want you to start thinking of risk as a *two-sided phenomenon*—the range of possibilities captures outcomes that are both better and worse compared to your expectations. Understanding probabilities and risk is key to good decision-making, but before we can move to more advanced topics, we must get familiar with the concept of expected outcomes.

How Expected Outcomes Shape Our Choices: The Unexpected Case for Freedom

When we talk about risk, we also have to consider the idea of the *expected outcome*, critical to sound judgment and decision-making. It is the bridge between action and consequence. Consider, for a moment, a simple decision: climbing a tall tree and standing on a precarious branch. You know the risks. The most likely outcome is that you'll fall and hurt yourself, perhaps break a bone. Sure, there's a chance you might keep your balance or land without injury, but such benign outcomes are far less probable. In this case, the decision is easy—you stay safely on the ground. The highly probable prospect of a painful fall outweighs the allure of more optimistic but less likely scenarios.

This process of decision-making, weighing risks and potential rewards, happens in our brains constantly. When we make decisions in uncertain situations, we mentally balance the probabilities of all possible outcomes, assigning different 'weights' based on how likely they are. This concept, known as the *expected outcome* or *probability-weighted average*, is the key to predicting consequences. For example, in a game with a 50 per cent chance of winning $30, a 30 per cent chance of winning $10, and a 20 per cent chance of winning $5, the average payout is $15 (simple average of 30, 10, and 5). It offers useful information about the central tendency within the range of outcomes. The expected outcome, on the other hand, accounts for the higher likelihood of the largest prize ($30) and equals $19 (calculated by adding the respective probability-adjusted outcomes of 50 per cent of 30, 30 per cent of 10, and 20 per cent of 5).

It reflects not just the possibilities but their respective probabilities (i.e., 50 per cent is much more probable than 30 per cent and more than twice more likely than 20 per cent). Respective probabilities vs. possibilities is a crucial nuance in decision-making. Consider a simple investment case: an investment strategy offers two potential outcomes—win $100 or lose 50. They are equally likely: it's like flipping a coin with a gain of 100 for tails and a loss of 50 for heads. We get the expected outcome by adding a win of 50 per cent of 100 to a loss of 50 per cent of 50, resulting in an overall probability-weighted gain of $25. This means that, on average, you would expect to gain 25 over the long run if you were to play this strategy repeatedly. Even though there's a possibility of losing 50, the possible, and equally likely, gain of 100 balances it out, such that the expected outcome over many trials would be a net gain of 25 each time you play.

While overly simplified, the framework above illustrates how our brains navigate life's uncertainties, calculate risk and determine which choices are worth making. This foundation is explored in the expected utility theory, presented by von Neumann and Morgenstern in their seminal 1944 work, *Theory of Games and Economic Behavior*. Their theory remains pivotal in understanding how humans weigh uncertainty and rewards, and has been supported by numerous neuroscientific studies. For instance, Timothy Behrens' 2007 research, 'Learning the value of information in an uncertain world', demonstrated how the brain encodes probabilities, updates them based on experience, and evaluates expected rewards.

But what happens when this intricate process breaks down? Degenerative brain conditions like dementia impair various cognitive functions, including decision-making, impulse control, and judgment, damaging the brain's ability to weigh risks and predict outcomes. Those afflicted gradually descend into confusion, often making decisions that endanger their health, not out of wilful recklessness but because their brains can no longer accurately assess the expected outcome and, hence, the consequences of their actions.

Now, consider this same cognitive deformation not as a result of disease but as an outcome of a socially imposed limitation on decision-making. The authoritarian regime I was born into behind the Iron Curtain worked tirelessly to control the flow of information, reduce the variability of social outcomes and limit the ability to envision a broader range of life's possibilities. Lives unfolded much like timid flowers under strict supervision, their leaves carefully pruned, growing only in the direction and as far as the state allowed. Its citizens gradually lost the ability to even dream about alternative futures. You simply cannot dream about what you don't know and cannot possibly conceive.

Imagine what this narrowing of life's expected outcomes would look like under our Monte Carlo simulation. In a free society, the possible paths of your life might spread widely, allowing for both mundane and extraordinary outcomes. Under communism, there was nothing but a central tendency—no place for miracles or even failures for that matter. All lives were tightly clustered, converging into a single line, drawn by the state.

Growing up as a kid in communist Bulgaria, I experienced this firsthand. Although I watched the Berlin Wall fall on television in 1989, Communism in my own country lingered for a few more years. Nonetheless, the sight of that wall collapsing brought with it an overwhelming sense of possibility—a moment when life itself expanded as the physical barrier between East and West crumbled. Before then, the range of potential outcomes in my life was starkly limited. I would likely remain in my hometown, following my parents' profession, never imagining alternative life paths...for the regime did not permit such dreams. It controlled the expected outcomes of not only our actions but our very imagination. Travel was restricted, career options were limited, and even imagining a life beyond those boundaries was dangerous.

Yet, when the Berlin Wall fell, everything changed. In the years that followed, still a child, I began to imagine a future beyond the narrow confines of the regime. I recall my mother urging me to leave the country as soon as I could—advice I followed before turning eighteen. Around this time, Radio Free Europe, broadcasting illegally from Munich, became a lifeline to the world outside. My family, like many others, would gather in secret to listen. Through the crackling static, we could hear news from the West, the roar of powerful West German cars speeding down open roads, and the rhythms of American rock 'n' roll. These sounds represented freedom, a world of expanded possibilities and expected outcomes that had been unimaginable before.

Looking back, I realise freedom is more than just a political concept. It's a psychological necessity for decision-making. If the brain depends on expected outcomes to guide our actions, then freedom allows us to imagine and pursue the most unlikely but extraordinary possibilities, bringing them closer to reality. To achieve something exceptional—a dream, a goal, perhaps even a miracle—you must first have the freedom to imagine it. And for that, you need a system that fosters, rather than restricts, the imagination. The fall of the Berlin Wall didn't just open borders: it opened minds. The state no longer predetermined the expected outcome of my life—it became open to the extraordinary.

Rule of Large Numbers: How Persistence Tips the Scales

The expected outcome, just like freedom, is a concept. You may not get the expected result the first time around. In the long run, however, after many trials, reality and expectations start to converge. In our simple coin game above, you won't get the expected outcome of $25 each time you play. Over many trials, however, your result would likely be around $25 on average across all the coin flips you played. Let's return to our 100-sided die. What's the expected outcome, rolling a die like that? I said earlier that when you roll the die, there is a 1 per cent chance of getting a certain number. Applying (multiplying) this probability to each possible side from 1 to 100 and adding them all up results in a probability-weighted average of around 50 (50.5, to be precise)—the expected return for our die. Let's start rolling it and keep track of the actual average result we get. If you roll the die just once or twice, you may get a 99 and 100, averaging way above our expected outcome. But what if you rolled the die one thousand or one million times? Over time, the die will land roughly an equal number of times on sides greater and smaller than 50, with the average result gradually converging with our expected outcome. This is the statistical law of large numbers: as the number of independent trials increases, the average of observed outcomes converges towards the expected value.

The rule of large numbers teaches us several important lessons. First, it offers an expected return as a goal we can strive towards over time, recognising that along the way we will face outcomes that are both better and worse than what we expect. The variability around the expected outcome in our 100-sided die is significant, and the range of possibilities goes from 1 to 100. Let's consider any number above the expected result of 50 as an upside (*positive* deviation from the expected outcome) and any below 50 as a *negative* fluctuation or risk. The variability of potential outcomes in our die is wide, but over time, the negative ones below 50 roughly equal the desirable outcomes above the expected average. Getting a 20, when you expect 50 is clearly disappointing, while 100 is a dream come true. It's similar in life. This dual nature of risk means that every downside has an upside, and every loss carries the potential for subsequent gain. The key is to understand and harness this variability to your advantage.

The second reason the rule of large numbers is informative is because it reveals a cognitive bias in statistical probabilities that can lead us astray. An unprovoked experiment delivered the first lesson about risk management in my family. My son M., five years old at the time, kept trying to climb the back of the sofa despite my warnings that he might fall. Of course, he didn't listen and managed to climb on top, grinning widely at me. I explained that he got lucky as the chance of falling was high. The more he tried, the more likely he was to ultimately fall. He continued unfazed but eventually fell on his fourth attempt. Throughout his efforts, he experienced a well-studied cognitive bias, commonly referred to as the 'optimism bias' or 'illusion of invulnerability'.

This bias occurs when individuals systematically underestimate the actual risk of a negative outcome, based on prior experiences where they got 'lucky'. A gambler who wins may downplay the risk of losing, though the odds always favour the casino. Extreme sports athletes who pull off risky stunts unscathed may feel invulnerable and try ever more dangerous tricks. Mediocre financial investors in an 'everything-up' bull market rally may deem their gains driven by superior investment acumen, taking greater and greater financial risks. My son thought he was a master sofa climber until he fell, luckily landing on his feet like a cat. The law of large numbers teaches us that if we make a choice with a poor expected outcome, we will sooner or later suffer the consequences, even if luck spares us at the start.

To further illustrate this point, we played a little coin game of heads and tails (with each of my sons when they turned 5). Heads, I win. Tails, he does. We started recording the results. Heads, tails, heads, tails, tails, tails. At this point, I asked him, 'Who do you think will win'? Confident from his three-tails-in-a-row advantage, one of my sons thought he would keep it and eventually prevail. We kept playing, and after about 15 coin tosses, I was ahead. This little game led to the first lesson I taught my sons:

Sometimes, you get lucky, and unlikely good things happen. Sometimes, you get unlucky, and unlikely bad things occur.

Or, to be more precise, if you play only a few times, you may get unexpected results, either positive or negative. The most important takeaway from the rule of large numbers, however, is that in the long run, the expected outcome prevails. If you flip a coin only four times, you may get tails on all four of them. If you flip the coin 100 times, you will get tails around half the time, which is what you would expect.

Change the Odds, Don't Rely on Luck!

I find profound meaning in this simple coin toss. I find hope after desperation and conviction that if I keep knocking on enough doors in life, one of them will ultimately open. Perseverance pays off. Fix the odds of the game in your favour through hard work, training, skill, or a natural gift, and even if you stumble, as long as you keep going, those favourable odds will ultimately play out. I have learned to distinguish between having the odds in your favour and being lucky.

As we just learned, luck is flipping tails four times in a row—a relatively low 6 per cent probability, but definitely possible. The expected outcome of a coin flip is that you get the same number of tails and heads (each side 50 per cent of the time). Over a large number of trials, the number of times you get tails will converge to 50 per cent of all, even if you start with a lucky streak.

In other words, luck is fickle. To rely on it is to invite failure. How can you change the odds so you don't depend on luck?

The first strategy is to keep rolling the die—a lesson in persistence and an antidote to reliance on luck. The more you roll the die, the closer you will get to the expected outcome, assuming it's in your favour. You can see this in action with job applications. We all know that applying to three jobs without getting an interview doesn't mean that we will never be able to land a new position. Eventually, as we keep applying, the expected outcome (a job offer), aligned with our skills and effort, will occur.

Another important strategy is changing the odds in your favour. This is equivalent to increasing the probability of success and reducing the likelihood of failure, thus improving your expected outcome. Think of it as rigging a coin, which lands on the desired side more often than on the other. As you learn about the success of others, you will often find that rigorous training, determination, and an unwavering will to succeed are all key to changing the odds in your favour.

Preparation and perseverance with favourable odds will ultimately lead to success.

One of the most inspirational stories I have come across is that of former American world champion boxer Vinny Pazienza, portrayed in the 2016 movie *Bleed for This*. In 1991, Pazienza was forced to give up his title after a car accident fractured vertebrae in his neck. Doctors said he might never walk again, let alone fight. For months, Pazienza wore a halo brace screwed into his skull and supported by four metal rods. Despite the pain, he trained rigorously, determined to return to the ring. Thirteen months after his accident, Vinny defeated future WBC world middleweight champion Luis Santana, staging one of the most remarkable comebacks in the sport's history. He then knocked out former world champion Lloyd Honeyghan to win the IBO middleweight world title in 1993 with an 11th-round knockout.

In the movie, after he returns to the ring, a journalist asks Pazienza, 'What was the biggest lie you've ever been told'? 'It's not that simple', he replies. 'That's the biggest lie—a lie they tell you over and over again to get you to give up'. 'So, what's the truth'? she asks him. 'That it is [that simple]'.

While working hard and continuously honing your skills may not guarantee you success, it will most certainly improve your odds. For fear of failing, most people never try something deemed extremely hard or impossible to achieve. Of those who do, some won't be equipped to face the challenges. Many give up when they encounter hardship and lose conviction in their abilities. Persevere, and you have already significantly improved your odds of winning. Don't despair if you are still far from your goal after considerable effort. You can roll a die with five winning sides and one losing and still land on a loss. It is vital to not give up and to keep rolling the die.

Training and preparation are critical. First and foremost, do your homework. In finance, this is called 'due diligence'. It means comprehensively studying your investment target, its strengths and weaknesses, growth opportunities, and potential threats. Due diligence is like the strict training diet and practice runs of an athlete before a marathon, the endless rehearsal of each phrase, glance and gesture of an actress before the big show.

Such intensive preparation and in-depth understanding of the challenges ahead forge an important conviction in the investor. This conviction helps you persevere in the face of misfortune or temporary challenges outside your control and resist the temptation to 'sell' when the price of security declines, to avoid losses and the discomfort of being 'the only one who got it wrong'. Conviction is critical. Confidence, built through a reinforcing cycle of training and success, is a self-fulfilling prophecy.

In a raging storm, a ship can only stay the course and avoid being blown to pieces by the towering waves if it's built on robust foundations and operated by a skilled crew. Knowledge and preparation are the antidotes to fear, resignation, and lack of confidence.

Don't Be Afraid of Fear

Fear can be defeatist. It can cause you to give up the fight. But fear can also spur preparation. A child fears the dark lurking in his bedroom and clutches his mother's dress. He knows every inch of this room, but when it's veiled in darkness, there is a chance a monster might have snuck in between dinner and the warm bath. Fear protects us but also stalls our progress. Overcoming fear without addressing the danger that evoked it is foolish. If you turn on the lights and do find a monster curled up on your bookshelves, your fear will hopefully grow once justified, based on the knowledge acquired upon illuminating the room. And if you are to fight a monster, as knights in fairytales do, you'd better prepare your sword, shining armour, and a few magic spells. Fear disappears only when the monster is defeated, which requires you to fight—and to be prepared to fight.

If you have rigorously analysed the company you have invested in, and the price of its equity or debt securities declines, your fear is justified. Conviction in an investment thesis is not immutable or forever unscathed by the ever-changing world. It involves understanding the fundamental drivers of value, forming a thesis of how this value may evolve, and continuously testing this thesis as circumstances change or new information emerges. If circumstances do change, and our analysis suggests suboptimal returns or likely loss, we must change course and cut our losses swiftly. If you have a close friend whom you have supported and shared many happy moments with, but he turns his back on you in moments of need, perhaps it's time to look for friendship elsewhere.

Identify a situation in your life where uncertainty looms large. What do you expect will happen? Could the outcome be better or worse than what you expect? How can you transform this uncertainty into an opportunity? What steps will you take to tip the odds in your favour, turning risk into a launchpad for success?

Key Takeaways: Risk is the variability in outcomes, carrying both threats and opportunities. It's the pulse of possibility. By understanding and mastering this inherent variability, you turn uncertainty into a powerful ally. Remember, perseverance in the face of risk, especially with the odds in your favour, doesn't just lead to survival—it leads to success. To achieve the extraordinary, you must first imagine it.

Having grasped the dual nature of variability and risk—both as a potential threat and an opportunity—we're now ready to examine how averages and expected outcomes can sometimes be misleading. In the next chapter, we'll explore why focusing solely on the average might cause us to overlook important extremes, and how being aware of these outliers can lead to better decision-making.

Chapter 3
Fallibility of the Average: Embracing Variability

Averages make us feel safe. They are predictable. Reasonable. But here's the thing: the average is almost never what actually happens. If you're standing with one foot in ice and the other in fire, on average, you're fine—yet you're burning up. In life and investing, it's the tails—the extremes—that shape everything.

In the prior chapter, we established the importance of understanding and managing risk. It's time to consider how relying too much on averages and expected outcomes can skew our perception of reality and lead to suboptimal decisions. While our brains are equipped to assess multiple scenarios and assign probabilities drawn from experience, we are equally looking to simplify the analysis and find shortcuts. Attempting to assess all the nuanced potential outcomes of a single decision, let alone life's endless possibilities, becomes a daunting task, more likely to lead to indecisiveness or even confusion rather than a clear vision of the path forward. Understanding the central tendency behind a range of probable outcomes is, therefore, critical to assessing the most likely flow of events and forging an appropriate plan of action.

In investing, such a central tendency is often called the 'base case'. Financial analysts often develop models to project how a company—and therefore, investments in its debt or equity—will perform. They obsess over the base case, representing the probability-weighted expected outcome, a simple average, or the most likely outcome. For example, the base case for a relatively young, innovative company might be a significant 10 per cent revenue growth and profitability expansion for the next three to five years as it captures market share from competitors. The base case for an established industry incumbent would be a more modest 2 to 3 per cent growth, linked to annual price inflation and population growth, and stable profits.

Reducing the spectrum of possibilities to a single scenario simplifies the analysis of an investment decision but holds important drawbacks. By examining the limitations of averages and the base case, we can better prepare for unexpected events outside the norm in both investing and life.

When the Consensus Goes Wild

While the average is a powerful tool for data analysis, it can sometimes be misleading if not interpreted with caution. Every quarter, thousands of publicly listed companies release their financial results, and these are scrutinised against a consensus expectation—a simple average of available models by research analysts at investment banks. Typically, the consensus assigns equal weight to all research estimates. However, the result could be modified to rely more heavily on projections from leading financial institutions. The financial industry rightfully places significant importance on these quarterly results, which are vital for assessing short-term performance and emerging long-term trends. However, it's important to remember that while these consensus averages are a useful benchmark, they should not be the sole determinant of an investment strategy. Focusing exclusively on a base case, represented by a simple or a probability-weighted average, can obscure the underlying risks and opportunities *outside of the consensus*, particularly extreme or unlikely outcomes that could dramatically impact long-term value and performance.

The average can be easily skewed by extremely high or, conversely, low estimates and become misleading. Think back to the late 1990s, when internet-related companies with little to no earnings, some running with deep losses and others with no sales, reached astronomical valuations. Lofty expectations by many investors and analysts about the internet's transformational potential led to wildly varied growth estimates for many companies. These extreme expectations inflated the consensus average, tempting investors with the promise of huge returns, should growth expectations materialise. Prices soared, amplifying the buzz around a successful story, and the average expectations skyrocketed in a reinforcing loop. Outlier projections can meaningfully change the consensus base case, resulting in a tangible shift in investors' sentiment and risk appetite. Such euphoric bubbles inevitably burst when reality fails to meet the market's lofty expectations.

Take Zoom Video Communications. In late 2021, the public valuation of Zoom, offering the popular eponymous communication app, reached north of $100 billion. Usage of the Zoom video conference platform exploded during the pandemic, and an increase in valuation seemed natural. In a time when COVID-19 shattered our social lives, causing mass isolation, the ability to talk to people virtually, face-to-face and to organise group calls, resembling social gatherings, was astonishing. Financial analysts envisioned Zoom becoming a comprehensive virtual marketplace where users create and monetise a wide range of virtual events. The unprecedented surge in demand from businesses, schools, and individuals led to linear extrapolation of both the company's growth potential and the extraordinary circumstances of the time. Zoom's base case, according to the average of the exuberant analysts' forecasts, was continued through-the-roof growth.

However, as lockdowns lifted and in-person interactions resumed, Zoom's growth momentum normalised, and competition emerged. Life rarely moves in a linear fashion and neither do businesses. As of the writing of this chapter, in 2024, Zoom's valuation is around $10 billion or roughly 90 per cent lower than its 2021 peak. Averages could be wrong. Consensus estimates simply reflect the central tendency of the financial research community and can be further meaningfully impacted by outliers. Base cases become euphoric when the market is euphoric and overly pessimistic when the market loses hope.

Don't Count On Predicting the Future

Throughout my career, I've compared initial business plans to actual performance three to five years later at top investment institutions globally. I can tell you: it is rarely what the base case predicted. Some are worse off, while others are much better. We overshoot or underestimate—two sides of the same coin. Precise forecasting over a more extended period is immensely challenging. There are too many variables and unforeseen events that could not have been anticipated two to three years earlier. Intricate relationships between seemingly independent events are easy to overlook. There are many risks we are aware of but cannot quantify, and many that we don't even suspect exist. A smart investor hopes to base her thesis and succeed in buying an asset on a conservative or readily achievable scenario, with a greater chance of outperformance. Only inexperienced investors believe they can accurately and consistently predict actual future developments, even several months to a year later. Only the fortunate ones do.

Especially when there are so many wildly different potential outcomes! Consider our metaphorical die with 100 sides—a die with a much wider variability than normal (100 potential outcomes vs. 6 on a regular die). You'd recall that we get the average expected outcome of approximately 50 for this die by multiplying each potential outcome from 1 to 100 by its probability of occurrence (1 per cent for each side of the die) and then summing them up. It's important to understand that while the expected outcome of the die is 50, you'll rarely roll that *precise* number—statistically, only once in a hundred rolls. You might get close sometimes (rolling a 52 or a 49) or you might be way off (rolling a 97 or a 6). The higher the variability of outcomes, the less likely it becomes for the exact expected outcome to play out. This is as true for a complex multi-year financial investment as it is for something so multi-faceted and fickle as life.

You rarely get the average expected outcome. Things are either a little or much worse, or a little or much better.

Fallibility of the Average: Embracing Variability

The Base Case Can Lead You Astray

While averages provide a useful framework, they fail to account for the impact of alternative scenarios or extremes that can drastically alter outcomes.

Imagine this: a patient arrives at the emergency room where you are on duty, clutching their chest, struggling to breathe, and overwhelmed with fatigue. These symptoms immediately suggest to you a heart attack—Acute Coronary Syndrome (ACS)—the most common and urgent diagnosis when blood flow to the heart is blocked. But here's the critical challenge: these same symptoms could also point to a Pulmonary Embolism (PE), a life-threatening clot in the lungs, or an Aortic Dissection, a tear in the aorta that could lead to catastrophic internal bleeding.

The danger lies in assuming the most likely diagnosis is the only one. Blood thinners, for example, might be life-saving for a heart attack or PE, but in the case of an Aortic Dissection, they could prove lethal, worsening a patient's internal bleeding. In medicine, it's not just about acting fast: it's about considering every possibility, even if less likely, with equal scrutiny. The implications of being wrong are simply too severe. The base case doesn't always play out, and sometimes, doing what's right for the most obvious diagnosis can have devastating consequences if another condition is the actual cause. A good investor approaches decisions much like an experienced physician: arriving at a central diagnosis is important. Avoiding devastating outcomes, however, requires careful consideration of less likely alternative scenarios.

In life, it's equally important to avoid adhering blindly to what appears to be the expected outcome. Imagine you've been in a long-term relationship. Things feel comfortable and stable—there are no major issues, and it's the path you've been on for a couple of years. The base case, the most obvious outcome, is to keep moving forward together, maybe even take the next big step, like getting engaged or moving in. After all, you've invested so much time and energy into this relationship, and on the surface, it seems like a natural progression.

But here's the dilemma: deep down, there's a small voice telling you that something feels off—maybe it's a lack of true passion, a sense that you're not growing together, or perhaps you're holding onto it because it's familiar, not because it's truly fulfilling. If you assume everything is fine and push those feelings aside, you might move forward into a deeper commitment, only to realise years later that you're not truly happy. You've built a life on the assumption that staying in the comfort zone is the best choice, but the consequences of ignoring that inner doubt can lead to deeper heartbreak and regret down the road.

Sometimes, the right choice isn't sticking with what seems like the most obvious and convenient option, leading to the expected outcome. It's taking a step back, having honest conversations, or even taking the leap to walk away and rediscover what really makes you feel alive and fulfilled. In life, like in relationships, sticking with the base case—what's comfortable—can be the easy choice, but exploring other possibilities across the variability of outcomes, even the ones that are uncertain and scary, might lead to the growth and fulfilment you truly need.

Next, let's examine more deeply how embracing this variability, rather than fearing it, can lead to more robust strategies for navigating life's uncertainties.

Variability Motivates and Builds Enduring Behaviour

Following our discussion on the limitations of averages, it's crucial to understand that life doesn't always conform to expectations. Rather than always seeking certainty, deviation (large or small) from the average expected outcome shouldn't be feared but embraced. Such a mindset gives us the resilience and adaptability needed to thrive in an unpredictable world.

Fallibility of the Average: Embracing Variability

It seems as though nature, at the mercy of random forces and aware that change is the only constant, has turned life's unpredictability into the source of its richness, vitality, and resilience. Variability of outcomes is central to how humans learn, adapt, and form lasting decision-making patterns.

Behavioural psychology, particularly the work of B.F. Skinner, highlights the importance of variability. Skinner's studies on operant conditioning—learning through the consequences of behaviour—showed that intermittent reinforcement (rewards or punishments are delivered unpredictably) leads to more persistent habits than continuous reinforcement (consistent rewards). In other words, variability (e.g., sometimes you'll get rewarded for an achievement such as a successful sale, and sometimes you won't for the same accomplishment) is better than consistency (e.g., always getting rewarded for a successful sale).

In *Schedules of Reinforcement*, Skinner, and his co-author Charles B. Ferster, detail the results of Skinner's experiments. Rats placed in the so-called Skinner box, specially designed with a lever, were given a food pellet as a reward for pressing it. Initially, rats received their trophy each time they pressed the lever—a fixed reward schedule. When Skinner switched to a variable schedule, where rewards were inherently uncertain, delivered randomly after an unpredictable number of lever presses, the results were striking. Rats subjected to intermittent reinforcement showed a higher and more persistent rate of lever pressing than those on a predictable rewards schedule.

The power of intermittent reinforcement extends to humans. In a study led by psychologists Neal Miller and John Dollard in the 1940s, two groups of participants were asked to do a task (such as turning a peg a quarter-turn). One group received reinforcement every time they successfully completed the task, while the other one was rewarded intermittently. Researchers reached the same conclusion as Skinner: participants in the intermittent reinforcement group showed greater persistence in performing the task than those in the continuous reinforcement group. Intermittent rewards are more effective in building habits and reinforcing a learned behaviour than regular gratification.

These studies explain why gambling in a casino or investing in the stock or bond markets could be so magnetising, with their inherent volatility, the unpredictability of rewards, and the risk of losses. Unpredictability and variability could even hold the key to your love life. In her best-selling book, *Mating in Captivity,* Belgian-American psychotherapist and relationship advisor Esther Perel explores the importance of unpredictability and even risk in forging a long-lasting relationship. We all have a fundamental need for security, which we seek in committed relationships, but we carry an equally powerful need for adventure and excitement. However, generating such excitement, anticipation, and lust with the same person we look to for comfort and stability can be challenging. Parel claims that the caring, protective elements that foster love often block the unselfconsciousness that fuels eroticism. She invites her readers to 'introduce risk to safety, mystery to the familiar, and novelty to the enduring'.

The unpredictability of rewards and the risk of losing can generate immense excitement and an enduring craving for more—a subtle dance one must carefully choreograph, as risks can lead to real losses. Variability and the existence of alternative outcomes are powerful forces shaping our habits and behaviour. This is not to say that you should rejoice when things don't go according to plan. Failing can be beneficial, however, if it helps you optimise your behaviour and avoid even deeper subsequent losses. Both constantly winning or losing can strain a relationship. Sometimes, letting others win is critical to building a better connection, even if you can consistently dominate. Equally, occasional losses can make winning more rewarding and motivation—stronger. Think of a father with a teenage daughter who wants to run for her school track team. Every morning, they go running in the nearby park together before their days at school and work begin. The dad is a fast runner, a varsity athlete back in his college days who can easily outrun his daughter even today. Sometimes, he wins to motivate

Fallibility of the Average: Embracing Variability

her to work harder. Sometimes, he loses, so she doesn't get discouraged. This variability is key to his daughter becoming a better runner.

Now, picture a sports team that wins every game without fail. At first, it's thrilling—unstoppable, unbeatable. But soon, victory loses its flavour. It's routine, expected, and the thrill fades. Now, imagine they lose every so often. Suddenly, they're reminded that winning isn't guaranteed. They feel the sting of defeat and fight harder, making each win sweeter and more satisfying. It's the unpredictability that fuels their drive and sharpens their game. Winning only matters when losing is a real possibility. Conversely, if you lost every single time in a casino, you'd walk away. But with the occasional big win, you're hooked—because that little taste of victory keeps you coming back. It's the unpredictability, the chance, that keeps the excitement alive.

The bottom line? Variability is what keeps life interesting. The ups and downs, the wins and losses, create the thrill that makes the journey worthwhile.

Create a personal risk management plan: identify the key areas in your life where you might be relying too much on averages or expected outcomes. Develop strategies to prepare for outlier events that could disrupt these areas. What unexpected events could you face, and can you prepare an action plan in advance? Now, recall a moment in your life when you lost something. Is there anything you gained in return?

Key Takeaways: Averages can be misleading if outliers are not considered. Develop a risk management plan that accounts for potential outlier events. Embracing variability nurtures resilience and adaptability, which are essential to achieving success.

Chapter 4
Avoid the Snake Eyes

You can play a great game and still lose. How often have you made plans, prepared meticulously, only for something unexpected to derail them? While variability is natural and even desirable, extreme variability is disruptive and hampers our ability to plan. Imagine life as a daily roll of multiple dice with billions of possibilities. They collide, spin around, eventually settle and voilà! That's the luck of the draw for you that day.

Some dice rolls lead to marvellous outcomes, like stumbling upon the love of your life in a small café, turning 18 in Europe in the year 2000 as opposed to 1939 or receiving a bunch of Bitcoins as a present for your birthday by a corky friend when they were still trading at around one or two dollars per unit. Other outcomes are bad, and some are extremely rare and catastrophic. When I discuss probabilities with my sons, I call these rare and devastating rolls *snake eyes* (when two dice turn up one spot each, the poorest outcome in the game of craps). The importance of avoiding losses, such calamitous outcomes in particular, is a recurring theme throughout the book and a cornerstone of the decision-making framework it presents.

The worst possible outcome for anyone (with some unfortunate exceptions) is death. In the US, approximately 1 in 500 people die in pedestrian accidents, 1 in roughly 55,000 from a dog attack and about the same proportion from a hornet, bee, or wasp stings (*Injuryfacts.nsc.org*). The good news is that while such accidents do happen, they are rare, and life expectancy at birth in OECD countries today is above 80 years.

No Moral Fairness

Sometimes, bad things happen to good people and good things to bad. You can be a great father and husband, diligent at work, saving money for your family, only to be told you have six months left to live. Conversely, you could commit terrible crimes but escape to a peaceful life in a tropical paradise.

You can tell me God has a plan, every roll of the dice has a purpose, and those who deserved a 1 (assume the lower the number, the worse the outcome) but instead got a 100 will be rolling 1s for eternity after their glamorous life here on Earth is over. I won't argue with you. The purpose of this book is not to guess what happens in the afterlife but rather, while you are still rolling your dice here, in this casino.

A childhood friend, Taron, had immigrated from Armenia to my home country with his parents and sister (I recall having a crush on her), hoping for a better life. Industrious, humble, hard-working people. One day, when I was 10, there was a heavy downpour. It filled the drains, and water flowed down the streets in my neighbourhood. Some wise guy decided to use an electric soldering iron outside, water flowing all around. The machine, electrical current passing through it, touched the water. Taron and his family passed by at that very moment. His father was electrocuted on the spot. His mother followed, trying to pull her husband away, the electric current tightening her clutch on him. Taron wanted to save them both and died that day. His sister froze in fear at a distance and survived. I don't know what happened to her after. They all rolled snake eyes that day. Sometimes terrible things happen to good people.

There is no moral fairness in dice rolls. With chance events, getting a 100 is as likely as getting a 1 or a 50. At the same time and for the same reason—there is hope. If the dice roll spared you snake eyes, you simply keep rolling. The next roll could be a winner. The purpose of this book is to create a proactive strategy that helps you improve your odds of getting a 100, while reducing the risk of an outcome in the bottom half, particularly close to 1.

Are You Rolling Dice or Flipping a Coin?

Can we actively avoid snake eyes, given how rare and unpredictable they are? While rare, they are often not entirely random but predicated on our actions and choices, which may massively increase the otherwise low probability of a disastrous outcome. If you are driving your car well above the speed limit in a densely populated city after a few drinks, you may be flipping a coin with snake eyes on one side instead of rolling 100-sided dice. When rolling two 100-sided dice, you will, on average, get snake eyes once in 10,000 rolls, a tiny probability. But if you're flipping a coin with snake eyes on one side, you will get them half the time—an enormous risk for something disastrous to happen. Most people will avoid taking a risk with high perceived probability and devastating consequences. This is a simple self-preservation instinct.

The problem is that high-impact risks are often much higher probability than initially perceived. You think you are rolling dice with at least 100 faces when you are really flipping a coin. Whenever you are taking a risk with potentially devastating consequences, however small that risk may feel, always ask yourself:

'Are you rolling dice or flipping a coin'?

While Taron and his family had little control over what happened, the man who decided to use an electric soldering iron while surrounded by water made a preventable mistake. He thought he was rolling dice, each with a very large number of sides, but was really flipping a coin. He got snake eyes, too. Conclusion? Don't flip a coin with disaster stamped on one side. Carefully analyse embedded risks and respective probabilities. Sometimes, your gut feeling is your best guide: if the game feels too risky and the consequences can be catastrophic, perhaps it's best not to play.

The man's actions had a clear risk and should have set off alarm bells and flashing red lights. It's not only the probability itself that is important in decision-making, but the severity of its impact. Betting $100 that you will not roll a 1 with a single, 6-sided die and losing the bet is probably something you can get over. Playing Russian roulette with a six-cartridge revolver carries the same probability of failure, but I sure hope you would think twice before taking a chance at it.

Understand the risk embedded in your choices and the magnitude of the potential impact. And, at all costs, avoid situations where, if you lose, you lose it all.

No Guarantees

Even if you don't take foolish risks, you may not be able to avoid snake eyes because the totally unexpected may occur. Rare freak accidents are generally outside our control, and we do not typically consider them within the range of possible outcomes in any scenario. Imagine living through even a single day, contemplating and agonising over all the possible ways, however unlikely, we could get hurt or even die within the next 24 hours. What a joyless day that would be, gripped with fear of an imminent disaster striking. And when disaster strikes, there is not much we could do.

I once invested personally in the buyout of a top automotive collision repair company. The previous buyout had delivered excellent returns, and with two major global funds leading the new deal, success seemed guaranteed. The business was robust, thriving when times were good and resilient in downturns—after all, people always drive, and accidents do happen. The idea that driving could stop entirely seemed absurd and not worth any serious consideration. Then, COVID-19 struck. Roads emptied, repairs plummeted, and the company's debt became a burden too great to bear. My investment suffered a severe blow (nothing, of course, compared to the devastating human cost of the pandemic). This experience drove home a vital lesson: even the most unlikely risks can materialise.

A Window of Many Colours

In investing, as in life, safeguarding against potential catastrophes is essential, no matter how improbable they may seem. There are risks so profound they can knock us completely off course or out of the game for good. The key to resilience is simple but powerful: to the best of your abilities, make sure potential outcomes, no matter how rare, are never devastating. And if something could be devastating, make it so rare, it's almost unthinkable. This is the art of protection, a way to build our lives and portfolios so that we can take a hit and still stay strong.

In investing, this typically means diversification. While I lost all the money I invested in the collision repair business, I had only bet a small fraction of my total savings. I took a major hit on this individual position, but overall, the impact was contained. The real power of diversification, however, shines beyond finance.

Think of life as an intricate stained-glass window, each pane a different colour and shape, representing the elements that bring richness and strength to who you are. One pane might be career, vibrant and clear; another, relationships, glowing warm and steady; others, health, passions, creativity. When the light shines through, these pieces create a beautiful, resilient whole—a window that captures and reflects life's many colours.

Now, imagine a stone is hurled at the window. If your life is made up of just one large pane, a single hit can shatter it entirely, leaving nothing but fragments. Picture someone who pours everything into their career, relying solely on that for identity and meaning. One day, they lose that job, and the mirror shatters, leaving a distorted, fractured world behind. But when each part of your life is a separate, carefully crafted piece, the window can endure even if one pane cracks. Yes, there's a fracture, maybe even a small hole, but the whole remains intact, the other colours shining to fill the gaps, giving you time and strength to heal and rebuild. You can repair that one pane, knowing the rest of your window—the rest of you—is still standing strong.

In investing, this is the power of diversification: ensuring no single risk can break the entire structure. In life, it means building a mosaic, a balance of relationships, health, passions, and work, so you're never defined by a single part. When your life is a window of many colours, it can weather life's storms with grace.

In both investing and life, the rule is the same: spread your bets and fortify every corner of your life. Because when you're built this way, life can't take you down with a single blow. You're resilient, ready to not just survive but thrive, no matter how hard the world tries to knock you off your feet.

Surviving Snake Eyes

As much as snake eyes may have a devastating impact on our lives, I want to end this chapter on a hopeful note by celebrating the incredible resilience of the human spirit. Sometimes, even when faced with the harshest of circumstances, we can bounce back stronger than ever.

Take the story of Alexandra (Ali) Truwit, which captivated me at once. She is a former Yale competitive swimmer whose life changed in an instant when a shark attacked her—an exceptionally rare event—while she was snorkelling in 2023. Truwit lost part of her leg in the attack, but in a remarkable display of resilience, she saved her own life by swimming to safety. The physical and emotional pain that followed was immense as she grappled with the trauma and the challenge of adjusting to life with an amputation.

Yet, within a few months of the attack, Ali returned to the water and began training again. By September 2024, she won a silver medal at the Paris Paralympics in the S10 400m freestyle—a true testament to her determination and spirit. 'When you're truly faced with death and you understand what a second chance at life means, you want to make the most of it', she said after her victory. Truwit's story is a powerful reminder that, even after rolling snake eyes, we have the capacity to persevere and triumph.

Are there risks you believe are safe but could actually have devastating consequences? How can you prepare for this 'snake eyes' scenario to mitigate its potential damage? What does your stained-glass window look like? If faced with your own 'snake eyes' event, how will you build the resilience to bounce back?

Key Takeaways: 'Snake eyes' events are rare but devastating—low probability risks that can have catastrophic consequences. Proactively identify and prepare for these unlikely but impactful scenarios in your life. Resilience is key. No matter how severe the setback, like Ali Truwit, you can overcome life's toughest challenges.

Chapter 5
Bells and Fat Tails

People often assume the world is stable and predictable—an average day, a typical year, a normal life. But what if the most important events in your life are the least likely? In this chapter, we'll explore why the biggest forces shaping your future often live in the outer edges of possibility—and why learning to account for them may be the most powerful tool you'll ever gain.

It's time to move beyond our dice examples and deepen our understanding of risk. Effective decision-making requires assessing the full range of possible outcomes. Risk, in essence, is the uncertainty of the future and the divergence between what we expect will happen and what actually occurs. The higher this potential variability, the greater the risk and the lower our ability to predict the future. Averages give us a central tendency to aim for, but reality often lands us somewhere better or worse. At worst, we face the 'snake eye' events we discussed. At best, we get a miracle with countless possibilities in between.

Unlike our controlled dice experiments, natural phenomena rarely follow a pattern where each outcome, good or bad, has the same probability of occurrence. Remember our 100-sided die, where each face from 1 to 100 has the same 1 per cent chance of showing up, averaging out to an expected outcome of approximately 50? In real life, social or natural phenomena often follow a *bell-shaped* curve instead, where some outcomes are common and others are exceedingly rare.

If you're already comfortable with statistics, feel free to skim the next part. But if numbers make you uneasy—don't worry! I promise this will be painless and even fun. This chapter is the most technical one in the book, but essential for what's coming next.

The Bell Curve

Take a typical data set—standardised test scores, for instance, or hours of exercise per week. If you arrange them systematically, you'll often see a symmetrical bell curve, much like the one below. Most values cluster around the central region and taper off as they move farther away. This bell shape is a cornerstone of data analysis and risk assessment.

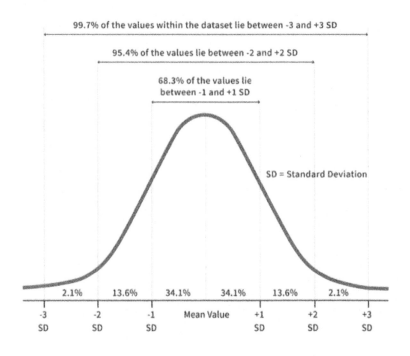

The higher the curve above a certain value, the more *frequently* that value occurs. So, if you place all the values in a dataset on the horizontal 'x'-axis, to the left and right of the average, respectively, the 'y'-axis, in simple terms, measures the likelihood of occurrence of a given value on the horizontal line. The average (or mean) of all points on our graph above is located in the middle, where the curve is at its height, implying that the mean is also *the most common* outcome. But the spread around this average is where things get interesting. A statistical metric called 'standard deviation' (SD) and notated with the Greek letter sigma (σ) measures how far values stray from the average and gives us a sense of the level of variability in potential outcomes. No matter what the data represents, the standard deviation remains a small number, positive for values larger than the mean and negative for values smaller than the mean. This little number helps make sense of anything, from exam scores out of 100 or the size of all living organisms to interplanetary distances. Think of it like baking cookies. If a recipe says to bake for 12 minutes, but your oven's heat varies wildly, some cookies will be burned while others are undercooked. A small standard deviation, close to the average, is like a well-calibrated oven—it ensures most cookies turn out just right. A large standard deviation? That's an unpredictable oven, leading to lots of surprises—some pleasant, some disastrous.

In our bell-shaped curve above, the average is the most frequently occurring number (and therefore underneath the peak of the chart), and the probability of occurrence of all other values slopes symmetrically to the left and to the right. This bell curve is called a *normal distribution*. The area of the chart within a given segment reflects the percentage of all data points located there. Many natural phenomena, such as human height, shoe sizes, blood pressure, IQ scores, the size of snowflakes, the weight of babies at birth, athletes' retirement age, or the lifespan of lightbulbs, follow a normal distribution. As the graph shows, most data points within a normal distribution (approximately 68 per cent of all) fall within one standard deviation (sigma) to the left and to the right of the mean.

As you move farther from the centre, the frequency of events drops meaningfully. Between one to two sigmas (standard deviations), you add another 13.6 per cent of all data points on each side of the mean, covering about 95 per cent of all outcomes. From two to three sigmas, the frequency of events gets extremely low (you can see the curve gets really thin), and you add just another 2 per cent on each side of the mean. Beyond three sigmas, we enter the realm of the extraordinary—less than 0.3 per cent of outcomes land there, making them rare and extreme. For investors, these 3σ events are where fortunes are made (to the right of the average expected outcome) or lost (to the left).

Here's a real-world example to showcase the concept of standard deviation. Say the average height of men in Europe is approximately 178 centimetres[2]. Most men are clustered around this average, with a standard deviation of 7 cm. Now, some men are incredibly tall, and others are extremely short, but 68 per cent of men fall between 171 and 185 centimetres (assuming normal distribution), one sigma (7 cm) to the left and right of the 178cm average height. Outside this range? Fewer and fewer men exist. Very short men and giants are at the opposite extremes of possible heights, but share something in common: they are both highly unlikely. Move beyond three standard deviations—below 157 cm or above 199 cm—and you find just 0.3 per cent of the male population. Pick 100 European men randomly, and you may not find a single one that short or tall.

Six Sigma and Tail Risk

You may have heard of 'Six Sigma' events—outcomes more than six standard deviations from the expected average. Compared to the 95 per cent of the 2σ, the Six Sigma percentage is 99.99966 per cent. This means that such events, to the left or right of the mean, occur in only 0.00034 per cent of cases or about 3.4 times in a million.

On the right-hand side of the curve (interpreted as upside from the expected outcome), Six Sigma events become miracles, while on the left, they're known as black swans (given how rare the bird is among its white peers)—highly improbable but devastating. The snake eyes we discussed earlier are black swans, floating amongst more commonplace daily affairs. Yet, at the end of that chapter, we saw the power of the human spirit to

---

[2] Some curious minds in science have wandered into far more exciting topics, measuring various other body parts within that same population with invaluable findings, though I decided after much deliberation to stick to a more neutral topic.

transform a black swan into a miracle. However exceptionally rare such 6σ events may be, they aren't so unimaginable in large enough data sets.

Take the world of manufacturing. Six Sigma lean manufacturing is a method used to minimise errors in high-volume production processes and continuously improve output quality to near perfection, implied by a 6σ standard deviation of less than 3.4 defective parts out of a million produced. The goal is to remove all but the very rare instances of errors and defects. Nothing you ever produce or do will be perfect unless you are a God. To achieve an ever-increasing level of precision, the Six Sigma lean process is designed to define, measure, and find errors, analyse and eliminate the root causes, and then continuously control for the achieved higher standards of quality. Production floor professionals trained in the Six Sigma lean manufacturing techniques are assigned belts corresponding to their level of mastery, much as in martial arts. There are white belts, yellow belts, green, and black.

In drug manufacturing, where billions of pills are produced annually, even a minuscule defect rate could affect thousands of people. As of this date, Pfizer mentions on its website that it delivers more than 50 billion doses of medicines and vaccines annually to people worldwide. Based on the Six Sigma defect rate of 3.4 in a million, roughly 170,000 out of 50 billion individual pills could be defective each year, with far-reaching and devastating potential consequences. Pharmaceutical companies such as Pfizer go far beyond the Six Sigma defect rate, relying on quality control procedures to detect and remove defective products, even if they inevitably occur in any manufacturing process.

Some have argued that the Global Financial Crisis of 2009 was a highly unusual Six Sigma event. However, others would contend that it was actually predictable in the context of a long period of low interest rates and loose lending standards. Extremely rare events could, of course, also be positive in nature: think about the scientific theory of Earth's creation—way more unique than a 6σ event. Consider this: out of about 8.2 billion people living in the world today, Six Sigma events happen only 3.4 times per million or 27,540 times. If you were born in a small town or neighbourhood of 27,540 inhabitants, then the chance of you being born in that specific town out of all other places in the world is exactly Six Sigma. Recall Buffet's metaphor and imagine a big barrel spinning around and filled up with 8.2 billion balls, each representing one unique human life. Now, toss your ball back in. Close your eyes, reach out and pick another ball from the whirlwind of lives. The chance of picking the same life you were given initially is 1 in 8.2 billion. Think about it—out of 8.2 billion people, no one has your exact thoughts, memories, or dreams. That's not just statistically improbable. Your very unique existence—one out of everyone in the world—is, therefore, way more exceptional than a Six Sigma and nothing short of a miracle.

Looking at our bell-shaped curve, both the 3σ and 6σ data points are located within its thin edges to the far left or right. These edges are commonly referred to as 'tails' because, you guessed it, they look like tails. The risk (probability of such events occurring) associated with potential outcomes at those tails is called 'tail risk' and is a fundamental concept in the world of investing. In practice, when investors refer to tail risk or a Six Sigma event, they usually mean an exceptionally rare *negative* outcome to the left of the average (or the expected outcome).

To return to our men's height example, given that just 0.3 per cent of men are shorter than 157 cm and taller than 199 cm, ending up with anyone outside the 157 to 199 cm range in our randomly selected sample would be considered a tail risk. The 3σ tail risk is 0.3 per cent, and out of 100 people, you would not expect to find any outliers (0.3 per cent of 100 is only a third of a man!), unless you get unlucky. Increase your random sample to 1,000 instead, and you'll probably find 3 men shorter than 157 cm or taller than 199 cm (0.3 per cent of 1,000 is 3). Your tail risk will likely play out, given a large enough sample. You may see zero if you are lucky or more than 3 if you are unlucky, but the expected number of men outside your desired height range would be 3. *The larger the dataset, the more likely it is that tail risks play out, and rare events actually show up.*

Continuous Improvement

The methodology to reach Six Sigma level of excellence in manufacturing is based on the principles of continuous improvement—constantly looking for ways to make incremental improvements that reduce the likelihood of errors. I suggest you apply the same principles of continuous improvement from the Six Sigma lean manufacturing philosophy to your personal growth. My experience investing in the healthcare space and touring many highly specialised drug manufacturing facilities designed to eliminate any possible contamination or production defect taught me an important lesson. Whether you are optimising a production process or improving your health and performance in any aspect of life, the path to success is the same: define your goal, eliminate inefficiencies, and continuously improve.

Let's take a practical example (perhaps unimaginative, but one that likely resonates with most of us). Say you want to lose weight. Using the Six Sigma lean optimisation method:

1. Define and measure: Set a clear goal (lose 5 kilograms or roughly 10 pounds). Measuring continuously keeps you accountable and motivated, allowing you to better calibrate your plan of action as you progress.

2. Identify and analyse errors: Maybe it's late-night snacking, too much screen time with picture-perfect social media photos, or emotional eating. Pinpoint your weak spots. Analyse and understand the root causes of your unhealthy lifestyle. Sometimes, this is difficult on your own, and you may require the advice of a close friend or a professional with an unbiased perspective.

3. Eliminate inefficiencies and continuously improve: Cut down on processed food and improve your diet, limit screen time, and start

exercising routinely—a bit more each week until you reach your optimal regime.

4. Control and maintain: Once you reach your goal, set rules to prevent slipping back and turn them into unbreakable personal principles.

This philosophy of continuous improvement applies to everything—from fitness to career success. Nothing happens overnight. Do not be discouraged: success takes time, determination, and repetition. Have a goal, work hard and don't give up. My kids must have heard this phrase from me a million times. Have you seen pictures of Arnold Schwarzenegger as a kid? He looks skinny and almost sickly. Nobody is born Mr. Olympia. Arnold started with broomstick lifts in a tiny Austrian gym, dreaming of becoming a body-building champion. He didn't transform overnight—he built himself one rep at a time. That's the power of continuous improvement. Some Six Sigma miracles happen out of sheer luck. The miracles we create are the fruit of the steady and relentless pursuit of excellence.

Writing this book, for instance, taught me I don't routinely get struck by divine inspiration. I waited for any, let alone divine, and it sometimes took months to arrive. Writing a book doesn't work this way. I had to push myself to regularly open my computer and write something, even if it was just a little or not particularly impressive, whenever I could sneak away time from in-between my career and family. I usually wrote late at night, on weekends, or on the train on my way to work. Then reread, edit, redact, and try again.

I cannot emphasise enough the importance of continuous improvement—whose impact is magnified immensely through the power of compounding—essential for the success of the Six Sigma lean manufacturing technique. Improve however little, but do it *every* day. Don't skip a beat. If you improve by 1 per cent from the starting point daily, you will be 4.65 times better by the end of a year (365 per cent improvement). If you factor in the effect of compounding and manage to add 1 per cent each day to where you are the prior day, you'll be 38 times better! In the world of finance, this is the power of continuous interest compounding: if you put one dollar or a pound in a bank account that pays you 1 per cent every day, you will have close to 38 dollars or pounds by the end of the year as you earn interest on the interest received previously. Buffet talks about this often in his public speeches. Even if you measure the increments of time in this example in weeks instead of days, you can make tremendous progress rather quickly.

Take swift action if you catch yourself lapsing into old unhealthy habits. I tell my sons the story of the baobabs in Saint-Exupery's *The Little Prince*, a book we have all three learned to love for our own reasons. In its magical world, seeds of baobabs infest the Little Prince's planet. He must make sure to uproot them regularly before they grow into mighty trees, their powerful roots breaking his tiny planet into pieces. Uproot bad habits in their infancy, before they take over and stifle the good ones. When you reach your goal, mark your success and celebrate it. Use the sense of achievement to boost your confidence and faith in your abilities. Schwarzenegger explains the secret to success this way: 'Do well and advertise'. Advertise to others, but most of all, don't forget to advertise to yourself!

Dispersion

Now let's circle back to investing. Financial models often assume that investment portfolio returns follow a bell curve, similar to our height example above. This implies there is an expected average return of, say, 7 per cent per year, though actual performance may equally likely end up above or below the mean, and extreme outcomes are less likely to occur.

Understanding the expected return alone is insufficient to make an optimal financial—or any other—decision. You have to understand the *shape* of the curve, its dispersion, standard deviation, and tail risks.

Focusing on tail risks as opposed to merely the expected return is perhaps one of the most important principles I have learned throughout my investment career. What distinguishes seasoned from inexperienced investors is the former's ability to think of returns not simply in terms of singular expected outcomes and averages (or the base case) but instead as a continuous curve reflecting myriads of potential results with varying probabilities of occurrence, flowing to the left and right of the expected outcome.

Why is this so paramount to effective decision-making?

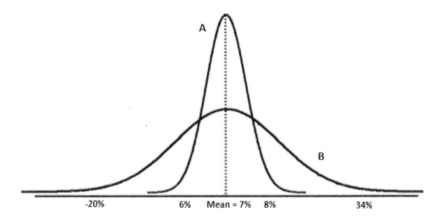

Let's look at the two curves above (not drawn to scale). They both have an expected return of 7 per cent per year. So, what is the difference between curve A and curve B?

Let's assume that roughly 95 per cent of the time (two sigma), annual returns in the historical period were between 6 and 8 per cent—returns are clustered only 1 per cent to the left and right from the 7 per cent expected average. This is illustrated with curve A. But if the curve is wider (larger dispersion), your returns could swing anywhere from negative 20 per cent to positive 34 per cent—symmetrically -27 per cent to +27 per cent from the 7 per cent average (this scenario is reflected in curve B). Can you stomach the ride? Which one would you invest in? Which one is better? If you assume that the curve is roughly symmetrical around the mean, the first important conclusion, which holds in the majority of cases, is that *achieving higher returns often requires taking greater risks*.

This principle holds true in life as well. If you want to see the world, explore its wonders, and enjoy its pleasures, you have to get out of bed and take all the risks that come with rolling out of its comfort and into the busy, bustling street. As Denzel Washington, who plays Troy in the movie *Fences*, says in one of his usual baseball analogies, 'You have to take the crookeds with the straights'. If you want to experience freedom and the highs of life—to stretch your potential on the right-hand side of the curve—you must embrace the corresponding risks as the curve extends symmetrically further left.

In our financial example above, you are likely to choose the investment option with lower dispersion (curve A) if you are averse to financial losses and looking for more predictable returns. Your return is all but guaranteed to be between 6 and 8 per cent. Suppose you are open to taking more risk, however, and can stomach more volatility in annual performance. In that case, you may be more inclined to go for the alternative portfolio (curve B), as long as you understand that you can actually lose money. Consider an illustrative distribution of potential returns involving a riskier, early-stage company, where your expected return may be to double your money. A reasonable upside scenario may see you make 4x on your investment, but you are also equally likely to lose all your money. It is, therefore, essential to understand the bookends of the probability distribution curve, particularly the left-hand tail risk. The latter may be relatively unlikely but extend far, holding the possibility of a complete wipe-out. One of my favourite metaphors, illustrating the significance of probability distribution around the mean, comes from legendary value investor and founder of Oaktree Capital, Howard Marks: 'Never forget the six-foot-tall man who drowned crossing the stream that was five feet deep on average'.

Let's talk more about two important characteristics of the bell curve: fat tails and skewness.

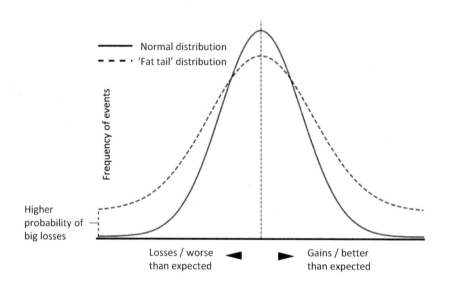

Fat Tails

The dashed curve above exhibits what is commonly referred to as 'fat tail' distribution. Fat tails matter because they represent extreme events that occur far more often than the normal distribution would predict. You can see that the distance to the base where the tails sit, which measures the frequency of occurrence, is higher in the 'fat tail' curve than in the normally distributed solid line curve. Understanding fat tail distribution risk is crucial in shaping investment strategies and decision-making processes, allowing us to better prepare for and manage the potential risks and rewards of extreme outcomes. Remember our clinical diagnosis example when we discussed the fallibility of averages? It presents a highly simplified world with only three potential outcomes: the diagnosis is either a heart attack, pulmonary embolism, or aortic dissection. If your highest likelihood expected outcome, in the middle of the fat tail curve above, is a heart attack diagnosis and you are contemplating prescribing blood thinner, then an aortic dissection is your very fat tail risk with devastating consequences.

Bells and Fat Tails

Avoid fat tail negative risk at all costs, particularly when it carries highly damaging consequences.

Keep in mind, however, that probability curves may not be apparent before making a decision, rendering performance evaluation difficult. Did the investor lose money because they got terribly unlucky with a 6σ event, or did they actively make a poor bet with a fat tail risk, which materialised? Or perhaps it was a misjudgement about how fat the tail really was? Does it make sense then to consider the distribution curve in decision-making if we cannot accurately predict it? Absolutely. It's the same reason we prepare and plan for the future, even though none of us has a crystal ball and knows exactly how events will unfold.

Here is a numerical example of fat tail risk. Look at the following number sequence: '0, 1, 1, 2, 2, 3, 3, 4, 4, 5, 5, 6, 6, <u>7, 7, 7,</u> 8, 8, 9, 9, 10, 10, 11, 11, 12, 12, 13, 13, 14'. The number 7 is the average of all numbers *and* the most frequently occurring number, but it still represents only 3 out of all 29 potential outcomes, or roughly 10 per cent. Imagine you put all those numbers in a hat. The chance of you *actually* pulling out a 7 is very slim: approximately 1 out of 10 numbers are 7s. While 7 is the most common number of all, numbers at the far left or right in the sequence are almost just as likely to occur, with many repeating twice. When you look at the overall set of numbers, there is an important observation that emerges. Even though 7 is repeated the most frequently (three times), the probability of picking a 7 from the hat is only around 10 per cent, while the chance of picking out any *other* number is almost 90 per cent, overwhelmingly higher odds.

The most likely outcome may be the unlikely one!

Alternative Scenarios

As we've seen, we don't always get the expected outcome or the most likely one and less probable events may occur instead. That is the reason for the need to always prepare for alternative scenarios: the expected scenario may not occur as planned.

Imagine you are a tennis player with an important match coming up. You may get to play against four potential opponents based on how the various stages of the competition progress. Assume the player you have the highest probability of facing is Red, and that's 40 per cent. Players Blue and Purple both share an equal probability of 25 per cent of facing you, and there is only a 10 per cent chance of facing Black. In the tournament's next stage, you are *more* likely to face Red than any of the other players. However, the combined probability of facing *any other* players is 60 per cent, significantly higher than the 40 per cent chance of playing against Red. *While you are more likely to play Red (40 per cent chance) than any other individual player, you are ultimately not likely to face him (60 per cent chance you face someone else).* And that has significant consequences.

Red has a weak backhand but a formidable forehand, while Blue and Purple have an excellent backhand but struggle with short balls. Black is superb with all the above but cannot return serves close to the centre. You spend all your time and energy practicing shots that send the ball hurling towards the opponent's backhand because Red is your base case. Yet, chances are you face one of the other players, and you are disappointed when all your preparation is rendered worthless. Your strategy falls apart. In life, preparing for just one outcome can be a costly mistake.

The example above highlights the potential consequences of not considering alternative scenarios in decision-making, emphasising the need for a more comprehensive approach. You see, professional investors make suboptimal decisions predicated on a base case, which holds the highest probability compared to the *other* possible scenarios but is not the likely outcome *overall*. When faced with such situations, making superior investment choices becomes less about defining and putting all your chips on a base case and more about picking situations and positioning yourself in a way that keeps you moving toward success no matter which situation plays out. We'll talk more about positioning later in the book when we roll dice and play backgammon.

The business strategy of scenario planning recognises the value of understanding alternative scenarios. You may think that scenario analysis has always been fundamental to business strategy and financial investing. Scenario planning, however, gained real prominence only in the 1970s and 80s. As Peter Schwartz writes in *The Art of the Long View: Planning for the Future in an Uncertain World*, it was then that Royal Dutch/Shell used scenario planning to prepare for an uncertain future and navigate volatile markets following the oil crisis of the 1970s.

Complex scenario analysis was hardly possible before the launch of groundbreaking spreadsheet computer programs like Lotus 1-2-3, released in 1983, or Microsoft Excel, which became the standard in the 90s. Before that, spreadsheets were, well, large sheets of paper where calculations were made by hand. I recall the former Vice Chairman of Morgan Stanley, Rob Jones, reminiscing about the times when he first joined the company, then a far smaller organisation. A simple error somewhere in the spreadsheet meant having to toss the whole darned thing away and start all over again, as subsequent calculations would also be wrong. You couldn't just change one of the inputs and automatically explore an alternative outcome like you can with Excel. Rob, an alumnus of my alma mater, Colgate University, and an avid supporter of the school, hired me to join Morgan Stanley's junior year summer internship class in 2004. He was a mentor to me and somewhat of a father figure during my time at the firm. I remember spending six hours with him in a car each year I was at the firm, driving from New York City to upstate Hamilton to interview for the next analyst promotions, gobbling up all his captivating stories, admiring how he managed to marry his incredible success with a sense of approachability and even humility. Bear with me as I give Rob a big thanks. I owe my life as I know it today to him. Him, and luck. He gave the job first to a young woman who rejected the offer and decided to pursue a career in architecture instead.

Even today, not all financial analysts consider alternative scenarios or the impact of potential bad or good luck, focusing instead on a single, most likely base case. If you use the principles in this book in day-to-day life, you will not only learn to make better risk-adjusted decisions but also begin to see the respective result as only one of many probable scenarios. You will start to focus on the *process* of making choices which lead to better results, as opposed to staying fixated on the result itself, the latter often a source of anxiety or unhappiness.

Skewness

Now that you've taken some rest from all that math, let me present the final concept in our statistics alphabet: skewness. It's core to the next section on Cheap Options, which introduces the guiding principle of this book. Skewness, in simple terms, reflects how asymmetric the data distribution is, and skewed distribution curves look 'tilted'. The direction of skewness typically reflects a long tail (to the right or left), which pulls the average value of all data points in that direction. *Imagine a distribution of outcomes where the negative ones result in small losses, while positive outcomes can lead to substantial gains; I call this a 'Cheap Options' distribution.* Investments, where the potential outcomes contain limited losses *and* the possibility of large gains, are sometimes referred to as cheap options[3].

The right tail (representing the gains) is longer, and the distribution is 'right-skewed' or 'positively skewed'. The illustrative figure below is the blueprint for the decision-making framework of this book. Negative data points cluster on the left side with relatively small values, while positive

---

[3] In finance, a stock option is a derivative financial instrument linked to an underlying share, where an investor gains when the share price increases above a certain level (called the strike price) but does not endure any losses if the share price remains below the strike price or declines further. The only cost the investor bears is that of purchasing the option. If buying that option is 'cheap' (the cost is low), the investor faces the prospect of limited potential losses (only the cost of buying the option), while enjoying material potential upside if the stock's share price keeps increasing above the strike.

values stretch out on the right side, creating a long tail because of the large potential gains.

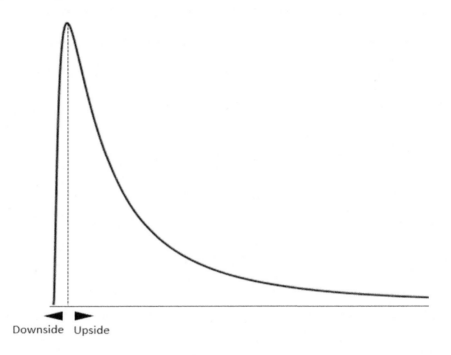

Downside Upside

Consider the following example. There have been times in the shipping industry when freight rates plummeted so drastically that certain types of container ships and vessels were sold at prices close to their scrap metal value and below initial construction costs. Such a dynamic can arise during severe ocean freight market downturns, driven by a glut of vessels and diminished demand. One striking example is the shipping industry crisis around 2015–16. In the years leading up to the 2009 financial crisis, ship orders surged in anticipation of robust demand. However, the market had shifted dramatically by the time these ships were delivered. Demand collapsed, creating excess capacity, a sharp drop in freight rates, and a scramble among too many ships for too few opportunities. Compounding the crisis was China's economic slowdown in 2015–16, which reduced global trade volumes. At its nadir, the Baltic Dry Index, providing a benchmark for the price of moving the major raw material commodities by sea, hit historic lows in 2016, with ships generating less revenue than the respective operating costs. In turn, this led to a material drop in the value of transport vessels, which could not be operated profitably.

This scenario underscores a powerful concept we'll explore in detail later: the connection between the Cheap Options framework and value investing, focused on acquiring assets at bargain prices. When you buy something cheap, at significantly discounted prices (in this example, at close to scrap metal value and below the cost of building a new vessel), the possibility of losing money and the extent of losses are limited. The lower the price, the lower the risk and extent of losses become. Yet, if market conditions recover, the potential for upside is immense, with a long tail of positive outcomes that can lead to significant profits. Over time, this asymmetry—limited downside risk and boundless upside potential—tilts the odds overwhelmingly in favour of success.

While this chapter has introduced the statistical and technical aspects of randomness and risk, it is essential to recognise how these insights can be applied to life decisions. In the next section, we will dive deeper into the Cheap Options framework, a strategic approach that uses the understanding of fat tails and rare events to manage life's uncertainties. This strategy helps us identify opportunities that offer *high potential rewards with limited risk*—key to making life decisions that minimise sacrifice and maximise gains.

Phew! That was a deep dive, but understanding these principles is like learning the alphabet—you can't read without it. Risk, uncertainty, and fat tails shape every major decision we make, whether in investing or life. Most people never think this way, but those who do gain an edge in navigating the unpredictable. In the next section, we'll apply these insights to build a Cheap Options-style framework for smarter decision-making—one that tilts the odds in your favour. A framework that is natural, psychologically desirable, and superior.

Are you making decisions based only on what's most likely, or are you preparing for the full range of possible outcomes? What happens if the rare, extreme event—the one you didn't plan for—becomes your reality? Are you positioning yourself not just to survive uncertainty, but to thrive in it? What small, daily action could compound into a life-changing advantage over time?

Key Takeaways: Fat tails drive the biggest wins and losses in life—ignoring them is not an option. The key to success is not avoiding risk but understanding and preparing for it. Growth, opportunity, and resilience come from pushing past comfort into calculated uncertainty. Small, consistent improvements, when compounded over time, create extraordinary results.

Section 2
Cheap Options

Now that you've mastered the concepts of randomness and risk, it's time to put them to work. In this section, we'll explore the Cheap Options strategy and how it can be applied to various aspects of life. As you progress through this section, you'll learn how to use this strategy to make confident, informed choices, minimising risk while maximising potential rewards. Alongside the Cheap Options approach, we'll draw on insights from strategic games such as chess, backgammon, and poker. These games teach us the value of thinking ahead, positioning ourselves strategically, and maintaining resilience under pressure—skills that are invaluable when applying the Cheap Options strategy.

What does cheating on your partner with a stranger have to do with investing in a start-up targeting a small and highly competitive market? The answer is that they are both poor decisions and hold the possibility of an immense downside with a relatively limited upside.

In the former scenario, you could destroy your family (let's assume you are not trying to) and bear negative financial consequences if the truth ever comes out. At the same time, the benefit is limited and, well, rather short-lived. Start-ups are generally high-risk, and a competitive market will make it even harder for you to survive. If your business fails, you will lose all your money, and if you succeed, as the market is small and full of other players, the rewards are likely limited. These are the types of choices to avoid in both life and investing. But what about the type of choices we should be making? Is there a framework for optimising your decisions? Yes, and I refer to such a framework as the Cheap Options strategy. In contrast to the above examples, this strategy champions choices with limited downside but significant upside, a type of defensive offence.

We often make suboptimal decisions that favour high-risk, high-reward choices. As we experience the pain of loss, our brains recalibrate and shift towards risk-reward decision-making that maximises long-term value creation. However, experiencing a deep loss at the start can be devastating, taking us off course and creating a self-perpetuating negative loop. Therefore, having a framework for making optimal decisions at the start is vital. We cannot control chance, or the choices life offers, but the Cheap Options strategy ensures we can stay in the race and keep chasing our dreams.

Moreover, in this section, we delve into the crucial concepts of sacrifice and trade-offs, which are fundamental to achieving big goals in both life and investing. Just as seasoned investors back-solve to determine the necessary steps to financial success, we can use back-solving in life to identify the sacrifices needed to reach our dreams. Here, the investments are the hours and efforts of your life, and the returns are the fulfilment and achievements you reap. Imagine crafting a strategy for life that is like a meticulous financial portfolio, where every sacrifice is an asset and every pain is a necessary investment, building character and resilience on the way to realising your most cherished dreams.

The Cheap Options strategy empowers you to make these dreams more attainable by allowing you to pursue high aspirations with a lower risk of failure. Imagine the power of knowing that each sacrifice you make is carefully calculated to bring you closer to your ultimate goals. By envisioning the ultimate outcomes of our personal and professional aspirations, we map out the steps to achieve them, planning our lives with the precision of a seasoned investor.

This section will guide you through this process, helping you navigate life's inevitable trade-offs with confidence and purpose, leaving you eager to unlock your full potential.

Section 2: Cheap Options

To explore the topics above and share what I have learned about optimal decision-making throughout my career in investing, follow me into the next chapters of this book.

Chapter 6
Chess, Backgammon, and Poker

Not all games are created equal.

Chess rewards calculation. Poker rewards psychology. Life? It demands mastery of both skill and randomness. Let's explore what different games teach us about how to play the one game that truly matters. Strategic games offer profound lessons in risk management and decision-making, mirroring the complexities of life and investing. Let's explore how these games can teach us to navigate life's challenges with greater foresight and skill.

Throughout this book, I lean on metaphors from boxing, martial arts, and various sports, and it's no surprise why: the discipline, focus, self-motivation, and perseverance critical to winning in competitive sports are also vital for investing successfully—and, frankly, for reaching any goal in life. However, when it comes to crafting a strategy for success, nothing beats the lessons we can draw from the combination of chess, backgammon, and poker. These games offer a rich palette of skills and strategies that mirror those necessary for success in investing and, as we will see more clearly in the chapters to come, everyday life.

As my sons grew older, the simple coin and dice games we played together evolved into these more complex games. Chess, backgammon, and poker are not just pastimes—they are masterclasses in risk management and optimal decision-making, both of which are essential in investing and life. Before exploring the Cheap Options framework and its applicability in day-to-day decision-making, join me in unpacking the wisdom of popular strategic games. They lay the foundational principles for navigating life's uncertainty—thinking ahead in 'what-if' scenarios, positioning strategically to minimise the role of chance, and maintaining unwavering conviction in your power to win even in the face of adversity.

There was a time when it was trendy for junior finance professionals to flaunt their chess, backgammon, or poker prowess on their resumes as a way of signalling their grasp of risk, probabilities, and strategic thinking—or perhaps their ability to read people. In today's world of 3D virtual reality games, social media, and a relentless barrage of distractions, the appeal of crouching over a board game may seem outdated. As a colleague of mine once quipped, 'Good at chess, bad at life'.

But I beg to differ. I still play two or three short games daily on platforms like *chess.com*. It keeps my mind sharp and adds a touch of competitive banter with opponents from around the world. Chess has been a part of my life since I was three or four, passed down through generations in my family. Growing up in an era and a part of the world where computers, video games, and even multi-channel TV were scarce in the late 80s and early 90s, backgammon was the game of choice. It was a constant in our household, accompanying almost any sit-down at the table.

My interest in poker also runs deep, though a mix of aversion to losses and limited financial resources in my early years confined me mostly to playing online with fake money or at the occasional charity poker tournament, where even losing was for a good cause. Now, I am trying to teach my sons to play chess and backgammon, though they resist at times, and I am holding off on introducing them to poker until they are a bit older.

So, what can these games teach us?

Chess

Chess is the quintessential strategic board game, with professional players devoting a lifetime to mastering its complexities. Like life, chess is vast in its possibilities. In the 1950s, mathematician Claude Shannon estimated there were around 10^{120} possible chess games, more than the number of atoms in the universe. Even when considering only sensible moves, the number of possible games remains astronomically large, taking billions of years to play them all out.

Chess mirrors life and investing: all three are dynamic, with your choices and strategy constantly evolving based on new information and the actions of others. Remaining flexible and reassessing your position after each competitive response is essential.

One of the most valuable lessons chess teaches is the importance of simulating various 'what if' scenarios to analyse potential outcomes, depending on your opponent's response. *If I move my knight here, my opponent will most likely move her bishop there, allowing me to capture her pawn.* But what if she does something different instead? Similar to investing, mapping out potential scenarios allows you to choose the best course of action. You cannot apply a Cheap Options approach to life or investing without understanding the options themselves. Even if you have a well-thought-out plan, you may not win against a formidable opponent, but you most certainly cannot win without one.

In investing, this approach can range from a simple 'what if' analysis to complex game theory simulations, much like in distressed investing, where multiple stakeholders with competing interests and varying degrees of power are vying for a shrinking pool of value. You end up playing 3D chess simultaneously on several interconnected boards. Regardless of the situation, having a strategy and carefully considering different potential outcomes is essential. The farther ahead you can plan for various possibilities, the better prepared you will be to handle whatever life throws your way and to position yourself optimally for the future.

Whenever I present an investment pitch or prepare for a public presentation followed by a Q&A session, I always have a detailed script with multiple 'what if' questions and discussion scenarios. Chess has taught me to leave as little to chance as possible. Grandmasters, such as former world chess champion Gary Kasparov, in his own words, could predict 3 to 5 moves in advance and sometimes 12 or 14 if forced moves are involved (those where your opponent has only one legal move to make, as the king or other pieces are trapped). If a move faces 3 most likely responses by your opponent, analysing just 4 moves ahead means evaluating 81 different combinations each turn (the first move has 3 potential move options, each of those 3 options has another 3 potential move options, representing a total of 9 potential moves; each of those 9 potential moves has 3 potential moves each, and so on). While this level of foresight is beyond most of us, thinking even one step ahead and considering its potential eventualities instead of resigning to fate can set you apart from the pack on your path to success in any venture.

There is another crucial lesson from chess: timing. Professional chess games are timed, and my favourite are short ones that test your ability to make quick decisions under pressure, with often seconds left for each move in complex situations. In chess, you lose if you run out of time, even if you are winning on the board, and victory is otherwise more or less certain without the clock.

Life today is also all about timing, with its relentless push for instant gratification. We live in a highly competitive world where opportunities don't last long. Savvy investors, constantly on the lookout, quickly snap up great deals at bargain prices, thus correcting attractive market dislocations. If you find a house that appears to be selling for a highly attractive price (the seller may be in a rush to get their money out) but remain indecisive and wait for too long to make up your mind, others will snap up the property and leave you searching. One lesson I've learned from tens of thousands of rapid chess games over the years is this: *it's much better to make a reasonably good decision on time than to seek a perfect decision that comes too late.*

This principle is painfully evident in investing. An investor may spend months researching a trade idea at an attractive price, only to see the opportunity vanish as others move faster, and the price increases. There is a big risk in overthinking. Sometimes, it is better to act with 80–90 per cent of the work done and take some 'leap of faith' rather than wait for perfection, missing out on valuable and perhaps rare opportunities. Time is quite often of the essence. We have transitioned from past eras, focused on creating the greatest masterpiece, regardless of time (perhaps what makes it timeless), to one where results *within a given timeframe* are paramount.

Take every opportunity to pressure-test yourself in stressful situations. This builds resilience and prepares you to overcome challenges when they arise. Significant stress can trigger panic with a rush of adrenalin, impairing decision-making abilities. As Mike Tyson famously said, 'Everybody has a plan until they get punched in the face'. The solution? Unsurprisingly, expose yourself to pressure or metaphorical punches, until muscle memory takes hold. It's the same in boxing, chess, investing, and life. The more you practise making decisions under pressure, the more confident and successful you'll become.

Try standing in front of a mirror at home with a stopwatch and deliver a two-minute speech you've prepared. The rule? No pausing, no restarting. If you stumble, forget a word, or feel the pressure mounting, keep going. Push through the discomfort, finish the speech, and then reflect on how you handled the moment. This exercise replicates real-world pressure—interviews, presentations, or important conversations where there's no option to stop and reset. It trains you to stay composed, recover quickly, and keep moving forward. When the stakes are real, you'll find yourself calmer, more resilient, and ready to thrive under pressure. Resilience isn't about avoiding mistakes—it's about powering through them.

Backgammon

Backgammon is a game of both skill and chance. Even the best player in the world can lose to a beginner, if the dice always fall favourably for the latter. Luck plays a critical role in life, investing, and this board game. As the saying goes: 'Better lucky than smart'.

While anyone can win a single game with sheer luck, long-term success requires real skill. This is similar to our earlier discussions: even the most skilful player can lose if luck isn't on their side. But luck is both a fickle friend and a fickle enemy. Sooner or later, luck turns, and over many games, backgammon invariably favours the better, more experienced player. The key is to make the best moves you can, with the roll of the dice you are given, whether good or bad.

If you have never played before, imagine the letter 'C' where the opponents' checkers move in opposite directions across 24 narrow triangles (like squares in a game of Monopoly), each trying to reach the respective end of the 'C' first. To secure what's known as a 'point' in backgammon, you must place two pieces on a single triangle, thus blocking it from your opponent. Leaving a single unprotected piece (a 'blot') exposed is risky—if your opponent lands on it, your piece is sent back to the start, holding up your advancement.

As the game progresses, players can remain peaceful and defensive, focusing on building points. Alternatively, they can turn aggressive, constantly seeking to hit each other's blots even at the risk of dismantling a defensive point and leaving a blot in return, exposed to retaliation. There is no singular strategy that always works. Sometimes, aggression is warranted; other times, a more defensive approach is best. The key is to establish tactical positions that optimise your ability to attack and minimise the risk of being hit, *regardless of how the dice land.* Our example on skewness comes to mind and buying vessels for close to scrap metal value. Sometimes, leaving a vulnerable blot to position yourself strategically for attack on your next roll makes sense, if being hit by your opponent is extremely unlikely. You have limited, low-probability downside but significant upside from a positional strength, should the blot survive your opponent's next dice roll. Imagine, the only possible dice combinations that would result in the blot getting hit are 4 and 3 or 3 and 4, respectively. There are 36 potential combinations, rolling two dice, so the probability of your opponent getting one of the two outcomes unfortunate for you is 2 out of 36 or less than 6 per cent, a relatively slim chance.

Remember our earlier discussion on optimising your chances of success? It's not about getting lucky but changing the odds in your favour. You can flip a coin and hope to get lucky, getting tails four times in a row. Alternatively, you choose to play a game with favourable odds. Backgammon teaches us the power of positioning—being at the right place at the right time. The following is an extreme example but one which neatly illustrates this point. Imagine living in a small town of a thousand people, which has amassed a lottery prize of $1 million. There are 1,000 lottery tickets for sale, and only one wins the lottery. Each ticket costs two dollars. So, you wake up at 4 am, go to the lottery booth before the 7 am opening time, making sure you are the first to enter, and buy all the tickets for $2,000. You are all but guaranteed to win the big prize, regardless of which ticket wins. This is the power of positioning.

Consider the following more practical example: a group of small coffee shop owners struggling to compete against a powerful global chain like Starbucks. Alone, their odds of success are slim, but instead of accepting the status quo, they pool their resources to launch a shared loyalty program called 'Local Perks'. Customers earn points at any participating café, redeemable across the network. This collaboration gives them a competitive edge, offering variety and community that a big chain finds harder to match.

By working together, they don't just hope for better results: they *change the odds* in their favour. What was once a struggle for survival turns into a thriving collective that draws loyal customers to all their shops. The lesson is clear—success isn't about waiting for luck—it's about smart positioning to create opportunities and stack the probabilities in your favour. In backgammon, investing, and life, you must make the most of your circumstances to position yourself most advantageously for the next move.

'Chance favours the prepared mind', Louis Pasteur once said, having made a number of discoveries through chance observations, which he then pursued with rigorous scientific examination. *You 'generate' luck by maximising the number of potential favourable outcomes.* Rolling the best possible dice takes luck. Positioning yourself for the best chance of winning, regardless of the roll, takes skill and effort. If you believe in the concept of destiny or karma, keep in mind that even in Eastern philosophy, karma embodies the link between cause and effect, where your conscious actions influence your future. The latter is not preordained by a higher power, but the natural outcome of all your decisions, accumulated in this life or past. Positive actions lead to positive outcomes, and negative actions result in negative consequences.

This ability to generate luck is an essential talent in investing, whether in publicly traded securities or entire businesses. Imagine you are a seasoned private equity investor whose fund has bought out a market-leading company. A deep recession hits one year down the road, and the business suffers. You are a skilled backgammon player who just rolled terrible dice. There is no sugarcoating it: your business will take a hit. But during the downturn, you do not sit idle. Instead, you optimise your cost structure. Knowing pent-up demand will create scarcity for the products once the recession is over, you invest in expanding your production footprint at an attractive cost during the recession. When it ends, you prosper and outpace your competitors who lack the necessary production capacity. You are well positioned, at the right time and place, ready to benefit from almost any scenario that could possibly play out.

The same principle applies if you lose your job in a tough market. Intelligent, capable, and well-regarded, you suffer from deep, broad-based cuts in your specific business unit. You do the best you can with the dice you roll. Perhaps you realise it's a blessing in disguise, allowing you to spend more time with loved ones or make that long-awaited trip you kept postponing. Don't just sit back and lament your bad luck or how unfair life has been. Go out, network with as many people as possible, brush up your resume, and reach out to friends and former colleagues. Optimise your positioning, and, eventually, the dice will roll in your favour.

Poker

The connection between poker and investing is clear: you bet money on hands you believe will win, on the basis of estimated probabilities under imperfect information. But poker differs from chess and backgammon: you don't necessarily need a good strategy or luck to win. In poker, it's all about attitude: you can be dealt a poor hand, remain unlucky in a losing position and yet come out victorious. All you need is to convince others that you hold the winning cards.

Of course, unskilled bravado usually leads to disaster in poker, investing, and in life. There's a fine line between bravery and stupidity. An astute poker player carefully calculates the odds, 'reads' their opponents, and uses psychology to gauge the strength of others' hands. Miscalculate, and you risk being called out by someone with a strong hand who has seen through your bluff.

In a world of imperfect information, winning often requires a blend of careful planning, risk assessment, unshakeable confidence, and unflinching conviction in the face of adversity. Sun Tzu's *The Art of War* emphasises the importance of strategic deception—appearing strong when you are weak and weak when you are strong. It's the art of navigating perception and psychology to improve your position and gain the advantage. This principle applies not just in warfare but in business, negotiations, and life. By the way, psychological manoeuvres to get your opponent off balance are also features of chess and backgammon through surprise moves, unexpected sacrifices, or the ability in backgammon to raise the stakes when your opponent is under the highest pressure.

But is bluffing cheating? In a world of opinions masquerading as news, AI-generated images, and social media, where perception and the number of 'likes' often outweigh substance, is deception immoral? Let's take a closer look.

In business, lying is unethical, and market manipulation is criminal. Period. It will end your career, destroy your reputation, and quite likely send you to jail. But in poker, you are not lying when you don't reveal your hand. You are simply not disclosing all the facts. No one asks you whether you hold anything of value. You never claim to have four of a kind, only to eventually reveal a worthless hand. If you bluff, betting big on a presumed winning hand, and your opponent folds, you win without revealing your cards. You signal the strength of your position through betting and reactions. But no one can force you to show your cards prematurely, disclose how you really feel, whether you are afraid or have true conviction in your hand. After all, you never really know whether you win or not until all the cards are revealed at the end or everyone else folds. Bluffing in poker is about betting on yourself even when the odds aren't in your favour.

There is always hope. No one in this world can tell you to give up or not bet on yourself. What is called a 'bluff' in poker holds a deeper and more nuanced meaning for me in life. It is the unwavering belief in the self, even against the odds. Conviction alone can sometimes take you farther in life than timid diligence. The day someone—or something—can delve into our minds, sift through our thoughts and emotions, and compel us to act in ways aligned only with the most probable outcome is the day we enter a dystopian nightmare. Living under a communist regime, I experienced first-hand one of history's dystopias as a child. Losing the ability and freedom to take a leap of faith is the end of humanity as we know it and a life without miracles. Our entire civilisation is built upon and fiercely defends perceptions that may or may not be likely or aligned with reality. Everything from the value of government-backed paper money to beliefs in the afterlife, the sanctity of marriage, and the vow of 'till death do us part' hinges on beliefs and hope.

In financial markets, value investing thrives on exploiting dislocations caused by sellers' excessive fear or exaggeration of risks. But you don't go back to those sellers and say, 'Hey, I think you're undervaluing this asset. Let me pay you a bit more because that seems fair'. As the ancient adage, commonly used in investing, goes: 'Beauty is in the eye of the beholder'. Distressed assets sell for bargain prices for a reason: they are complex, ridden with hidden risks, and a headache to deal with. If some of those risks do play out and you end up losing money, even though you thought you were getting a bargain, no one will come running to give you back part of the price you paid. Equally, if you have a strong conviction and you see something others don't, it is fine to win and generate profits or enjoy the benefits in life, as long as you have played by the rules. This is, after all, the basis for meritocracy. To me, poker celebrates the faith in one's self and the conviction to put your best foot forward, even when reality weighs down on you. Just as at a job interview after you've been laid off, you present the best version of yourself—dressing sharply and professionally—even if 90 per cent of your days are spent in sweatpants.

My advice? Go ahead and promote yourself. Bluffing in poker is a bit like betting on yourself, even when you've been dealt a weak hand with poor odds. In life, no one gives you credit for an unlucky draw. It's a race where people only care about where you are now, not where you started. If life were a race, what a strange competition that would be! Runners jump out of everywhere and claim victory, leaping from side alleys or right in front of the finish line. Some start at the back of the track in a wheelchair, yet still, they must compete in the same race. In today's world, people are often measured by their wealth, education, or social status. Some get the poker's equivalent of royal flush (five hearts: 10, jack, queen, king, and ace) in life right from the start, while others' cards hold nothing of value. Skill alone often isn't enough when you are dealt a poor hand or start from the back. To win, you must look, sound, and behave like a winner. You're in charge of your own self-promotion, and no matter the hand you are dealt, you can always bet on yourself.

Which game are you playing in life right now—chess, backgammon, or poker? Are you strategising long term, positioning for success, or betting on yourself against the odds? Are you rolling the dice and hoping for the best, or are you positioning yourself to win regardless of the outcome? If life is a high-stakes game, are you spending too much time perfecting every move or taking action before the opportunity slips away?

Key Takeaways: Strategic games teach valuable lessons in decision-making and risk management. Success is not about waiting for the perfect roll of the dice—it's about positioning yourself to win no matter how the dice land. Foresight wins the long game—plan ahead, anticipate challenges, and adapt your strategy to seize opportunities before they disappear. Luck may favour the bold, but preparation, positioning, and persistence create the conditions for miracles. Life is about attitude, and confidence isn't about having the best hand—it's about betting on yourself, even against the odds.

Chapter 7
Value Investing: The Hunt for Cheap Options

What if the secret to a better life wasn't necessarily working harder—but choosing better bets?

Most people think success is about intensity: pushing harder, running faster, wanting it more. But in truth, it's more often about selection—the decisions you make about where to invest your time, energy, and risk. In life, as in investing, the most powerful outcomes don't always come from grinding harder. They come from finding what I call Cheap Options: opportunities with a limited downside but a meaningful upside.

This isn't just a clever financial trick—it's a way of living. A philosophy. A survival mechanism. A quiet superpower.

And I didn't learn it on Wall Street. I learned it when I was 18 years old—halfway across the world from my family, with little in my pocket and everything to prove.

I consider myself a value investor, though I have always been a bit of a nomad in finance, just as I've been in life. I pushed myself to the limit during my high school years to ultimately win a full financial scholarship at a top US college—Colgate University in upstate New York. For this, I will forever be grateful to my alma mater.

How many doors did I knock on to make it happen? Around 40. My knuckles were bruised, but I needed the school to pay for everything. My parents, dedicated physicians working within a crumbling post-communist healthcare system, faced the hardship of economic collapse and hyperinflation. At the time, they could barely afford to pay the application fees, let alone cover tens of thousands of dollars per year for a top-notch private education. I was left to pay a couple of thousand in fees for my studies, accommodation, and board. I traded my meal plan for cash, cooked on my own, and cut costs wherever I could. To make ends meet and afford a trip home overseas, I worked multiple part-time jobs on campus—tutoring in German and economics, fixing computers, and working at the library and post office. My minor in German led me to study for a semester abroad in Freiburg, in the south of Germany, where I picked up jobs as a marketing rep and a bartender. The latter was low-paying, but with free drinks throughout the night, my choice of music, and the chance to return empty bottles for cash, it felt like a win.

College was the first time I earned real money, and the satisfaction was unmatched. Seeing that first pay cheque at 18 felt like tasting the sweetest fruit from a tree I had grown myself.

I vividly recall once fixing a computer for a student at his campus apartment while he and his girlfriend made out behind me. In that moment, I was invisible—unable to disturb them, perhaps even if I tried. But it was a turning point: I realised I had nothing to lose and everything to gain. If I wanted to achieve my goals, I had to make myself seen by becoming the best at whatever I did.

Within four years of college, I graduated amongst the top five students in my class and secured a coveted summer internship on Wall Street. After gruelling 110+-hour weeks, I landed my first full-time job at Morgan Stanley. I was living the American Dream, but it did not come without sacrifice. Each dollar and minute were meticulously planned and stretched to their limit. To save time and eke out 20 minutes of sleep between classes, homework, and my on-campus jobs, I often ran from my last class to my dorm. I'd fall asleep the moment my head hit the pillow. It was rough, and I felt out of place in a school with some of the wealthiest kids in the country.

Coming from a world so different, far away, and foreign—I was an outsider. But I was social, active in the community and knew how to handle my liquor in the brutal winters of upstate New York, earning the respect and friendship of my peers. I hid behind my cocky-funny demeanour and wrapped it tightly with my academic success. By the time I started my first job on the 32nd floor of Morgan Stanley's Times Square building, I had learnt that hard work, grit, and success are inseparable. What was that famous advice from Schwarzenegger? 'Work like hell and advertise'. I did both.

After a few years there and at a growth-focused private equity fund in New York, I spent the next decade changing continents and careers, trying to find my path while never giving up on my determination. I dabbled in a start-up idea and ultimately launched a London-based career in distressed debt, corporate insolvencies, and special situations with Blackstone and Carlyle, two of the world's preeminent financial institutions. Eventually, I joined a prominent global hedge fund focused on multi-strategy investments in publicly traded securities. Within my current position, I am privileged to work alongside an extraordinary team whose insights and collaborative spirit enriched my understanding of both equity and debt capital markets, providing me with an exceptional breadth of experience. As a dedicated distressed investor, I remember joking when asked what I did for a living: 'I do what Richard Gere did in *Pretty Woman*'. It sounded funny, but it was also true. Don't tell me if you've never watched that movie. It will make me feel really old.

My journey into distressed investing was accidental, spurned by the Euro crisis of 2011. With an MBA degree from the INSEAD Business School but no real experience in Europe, I pivoted away from growth buy-outs into distressed debt and special situations value investing in London, capitalising on the abundance of struggling businesses in need of advice or capital.

Defensive Offense with a Margin of Safety

Value investing is all about finding assets at bargain valuations, not necessarily at low prices but below their intrinsic value. Within value investing, the field of distressed debt and special situations focuses on finding such bargains amongst the ruins of financially and operationally challenged businesses in need of a turnaround and business resuscitation. Risk, specifically the risk of principal loss, is predominantly a function of price. At the extreme, if you have $1,000 to invest and you buy a stock or a bond for nothing, you have no chance of losing any of your starting balance. If you, on the other hand, haggle over a rug in the Grand Bazaar of Istanbul, and a skilful salesman convinces you to buy his Persian rug for $1,500, which you could have found for only $1,000 in nearby stores, you have lost $500 at the start. If you buy that same type of rug for $750 from a store that's liquidating all its stock and offering big discounts, you have made an excellent bargain. (Most often, however, we do not control the price, as the market determines the latter. While we may wish to bid $750 for the rug with a price tag of $1,500, greater fools may be willing to pay the excessive price, which means you are unlikely to drive a good bargain. In those cases, the best choice is not to buy and walk away.)

Imagine, though, that you took advantage of the forced selling opportunity and bought the rug from the liquidating store. You just paid $250 below the market value of $1,000 that market participants are willing to pay. The gap of $250 between what you paid ($750) and the true underlying value of the rug ($1,000) represents your 'margin of safety'. The term, coined in the 1940s by authors Benjamin Graham and David Dodd in their book *The Intelligent Investor* and later explored in-depth in the eponymous book by one of the profession's most notable representatives, Seth Klarman, is central to value investing. 'Margin of safety' is the buffer you have before you start to lose money, protecting you from poor luck, miscalculations in your thesis, or any other expected or unforeseen adverse impact.

Within value investing, purchasing securities of financially distressed companies allows for unique bargains at a significant margin of safety. Think about buying cargo vessels at scrap metal value. We discussed earlier how achieving higher returns typically requires taking greater risks. When a company is in financial distress, existing investors, fearful of ever-deepening financial losses, are often willing to sell their positions at material discounts. Market efficiency breaks down, offering distressed debt investors a rare opportunity for a 'free lunch': a chance to get an outsized financial return, while at the same time minimising the risk of a loss—the very essence of a cheap option. Fundamentally, value investing is the art of defensive offence: the focus is on protecting against losses, while actively positioning to take advantage of winning opportunities.

The Blemished Cake

One way to describe distressed debt investing is in the following example. Imagine you are the owner of a bakery. As you arrange the different cakes in the refrigerator window, you bump one of them against the edge, denting its beautiful glazing. It's ruined. It's delicious, but customers won't buy it because of its blemish. At the same time, your next-door neighbour's daughter is running a lemonade stand for the summer and wants to add cake to her offering. She comes in, looks at all the cakes, notices the dent on one of them and shrewdly but unashamedly offers you a mere third of the original price. Begrudgingly, you agree, knowing you are unlikely to sell it today and would have to throw it away if it remains unsold by tomorrow. You need to make a swift decision or risk getting nothing for the cake by the end of the day. So, you take a $7 haircut from the original price of $10 and sell it to the girl for $3. She cuts it into 10 pieces. Then, she eats the piece with the dent and puts a price tag of $1 on each of the remaining 9 pieces. Within a few hours, she's sold all 9 pieces, tripling her original $3 investment. She's had her cake *and* eaten it.

The Underwater Home

With the relative simplicity of understanding the value of a single building, the real estate sector offers another straightforward example of what distressed and value investing represents (and ultimately the theory behind Cheap Options). Imagine George Home buys a £1-million apartment in a prime area of London at the peak of the market, where a decade of low mortgage interest rates have fuelled a steep increase in real estate prices. He gets a 70 per cent loan-to-value mortgage or, in other words, receives £700,000 from the bank and pays £300,000 from his own pocket, which we refer to as equity (the value of all the shares owned by the sole shareholder, in this example, George).

As a friend of mine who bought a small motorboat once said, 'The two happiest days of owning a boat are the day you buy it, and the day you sell it'. George experiences the same: it's a painful ownership. Fast forward two years and the real estate market has crashed. Mortgage rates have increased in sync with the central bank raising interest rates. Recession and higher unemployment levels lead to a material reduction in rents. All of this results in the value of George's apartment falling by 50 per cent (a round number example for simplicity, representing a discount otherwise hard to imagine for a prime real estate property in London). His purchase is now underwater.

George tries to sell the property, but his agent, who he suspects has not done the best marketing job in the world, has come back with a £500,000 valuation while his mortgage is £700,000, meaning George's £300,000 in equity is now worthless. After several unsuccessful attempts to sell and recover any of his initial £300,000 investment, George ultimately loses all hope and decides to stop paying his mortgage, seeing the monthly payments as money down the drain (he lives elsewhere and bought the apartment as an investment; don't cry over him, he'll be fine). The bank, which holds security over the property, takes control of the apartment, which means the bank becomes the sole shareholder of the apartment by 'enforcing' its security—something George has agreed upfront would happen if he stopped paying his mortgage.

Jane Smart, Value Investor

The bank does not want to own an apartment as it is not its core business, so the bank sells it at an auction to Jane Smart for £500,000. Jane is a shrewd investor who expects the real estate market to recover and considers the purchase a bargain. She calculates it would cost her close to half a million to build the property from scratch on top of the enormous time investment and stress of doing so. To her, the £500,000 price paid represents a valuation floor, supported by the estimated cost to build a similar home somewhere between £400,000 and £500,000, and Jane is confident she cannot lose much even if the economy takes a turn for the worse. She effectively purchases the loan that the bank had extended to George for 71 pennies for each pound the bank has lent (she pays £500,000 to buy a £700,000 loan) and, with it, receives full ownership of the property. George has lost 100 per cent of his equity investment, while the bank has lost 29 per cent. Jane plays defensive offence, focusing on loss avoidance but preserving the ability to benefit substantially from any subsequent market recovery. Jane does not buy a flashy brand-new property in a growing albeit frothy market. She purchases the asset when the market is in turmoil and falling but at a bargain price with limited risk of meaningful further losses. She is in defence mode, but as we'll see, she is ready to 'attack'.

Another two years down the road, the economy recovers sharply. Due to a timely intervention by the central bank, mortgage rates are lower, and a new subway station gets built within walking distance of the property (Jane had done her research in advance of her purchase and knew the development plans would boost the value of her apartment). She hires a different marketing agency, fixes up the property, gets a builder to repaint the walls and makes some minor cosmetic changes, which are cost-effective but really freshen up the place. The real estate market has broadly recovered, and she manages to sell the place for a tad above the £1 million that George originally paid. Even after accounting for the minor refresh, she makes two times return on her original £500,000 investment.

This is the essence of distressed debt investing—buying assets defensively at a deep discount, fixing them up, and selling them at a profit.

How Assets Become Distressed

Sometimes, companies make risky bets, funded with significant amounts of debt, then fail or squander the cash away. I have seen second- or third-generation family owners take out loans to buy private jets, start completely unrelated businesses they have limited experience in, or buy cryptocurrencies that tumble to the ground. Investing in projects with limited due diligence and risk assessment often leads to losses, while companies are left stranded with pricey debt. Unlike buildings whose sturdy construction could withstand any recession, a distressed business facing financial challenges could fall apart and disappear. Why? It's a self-perpetuating vicious cycle: suppliers significantly tighten their terms or may altogether refuse to sell goods on credit, unsure the company can pay them back. Employees leave for greener pastures, while consumers switch to competitors, fearing the company may not be there to service their product down the road. Panic settles in. It's like a run on a bank in the absence of a government protection scheme where the faster you go to the local branch and pull all your money out, the lower the risk of being left with nothing. It's not a flawed logic from an individual point of view, but it leaves everyone collectively worse off.

This is the type of mess that distressed value investors look for and see as the best hunting ground for superior risk-adjusted returns. Fear and panic result in bargain valuations as the pendulum swings from excessive optimism to excessive pessimism. Distressed debt buyers like Jane Smart (also referred to as vulture investors given the state of their prey) scoop up the debt from original lenders at a deep discount. They often take complete control and ownership of the business (much like George's bank took over his apartment) in an out-of-court negotiation or through a court process, fix the company, invest in growth, and ultimately exit the investment through sale to the next buyer or a public equity listing.

The idea of creating a 'cheap option' is at the core of this investing style. The distribution of potential investment returns is skewed to the right: the maximum potential loss is limited while the potential upside is material. When she buys George's apartment from the bank, Jane Smart creates a cheap option. She knows the cost to build is around £400,000, in the worst-case scenario, and is therefore confident the price is unlikely to drop below that. The worst possible outcome represents a 20 per cent loss from the original £500,000 she paid, while the upside, as she experienced, was significant.

Staying Power

Jane possesses another coveted feature of distressed and value investments: *staying power*. Even if the price of the property falls below what she paid, she wouldn't lose the place. There is no mortgage coming due and no one who could force her to give the asset up. Jane has minimal annual property tax and some maintenance payments but could cover those and even make a profit on top by renting the property out. Even in the worst possible outcome, no one could kick her out of her investment as they did to George. She could *stay*. Sooner or later, she knows conditions will improve, and defence will turn into offence. Having done due diligence on local council planning, she knows there are plans to build a metro station near the property, typically leading to an increase in value. She doesn't know exactly how events will unfold, how long the new station will take to complete (if at all) or how much property prices in the area will go up. Exactly which scenario will play out is unclear, but she has purchased a 'cheap option'. Jane can afford to wait, *get paid* to wait by renting the place out, and ultimately double her money if things play out reasonably well.

A superior long-term investor does not focus on making consistently precise predictions about the future (she understands this is a futile or highly improbable exercise). Instead, she focuses on the distribution of potential returns and systematically invests in situations where the upside is far greater than the downside, while the risk of principal loss is limited. I call such situations 'Cheap Options'.

Consider the following example outside the world of finance. In the early 1990s, J.K. Rowling was, in her own words, 'as poor as it is possible to be in modern Britain without being homeless'. A single mother on welfare, she focused on survival—protecting her daughter, managing her meagre resources, and finding solace in her writing. Even as rejection after rejection piled up for her manuscript about a young wizard, she held her ground, defending her dream while keeping herself afloat. Her unbreakable belief in the saga of Harry Potter, already plotted out in her mind, gave her the staying power to persevere when so many would have given up the dream. Writing in cafes with a baby by her side, she preserved her core through grit and determination, waiting for an opportunity to strike.

When a small publisher offered her a £1,500 advance, she didn't just take the chance—she went all in. Rowling poured herself into her work, promoting the book with relentless passion. That single, seemingly small opportunity became the foundation of a billion-dollar empire, reshaping modern literature and film. Like a savvy investor, Rowling minimised risk by living within her means, endured tough times with unshakable determination, and turned an unenviable starting point into unimaginable success. Her story is a testament to the power of combining defence and offence: she protected her foundation when everything was at risk, then went on the attack to create success far beyond anyone's imagination.

Avoid Losses. Never, Ever Lose Big

Why is avoiding losses so crucial? What fascinates me about investing is that the market is shaped by the complexity of human emotion: cycles, bubbles,

Value Investing: The Hunt for Cheap Options

or excessive selloffs would likely not exist in an entirely automated market, devoid of human emotions and biases. Unlike interpreting complex human emotions, outcomes in financial markets are readily visible, easy to interpret and usually quick to show—you either lose or make money. This makes investing a natural lens through which to view broader life lessons and decision-making patterns. Here is a simple investment experiment to illustrate the point on losses.

Let's consider two investors: Reckless, and Steady. Reckless bets big, leading either to large gains or deep losses. Steady's investment style is boring, but he produces steady, reasonable returns. Give each a $100 to invest and let's compare their performance. Steady produces a 7 per cent annual return for the next 10 years and, by the end of year 10, turns your $100 into $198 or roughly doubles the initial principal investment. Reckless makes a risky bet at the start, chasing outsized returns, and loses $50 or half of your investment. To catch up with Steady, Reckless will need to produce a whopping 17 per cent return each of the next 9 years, almost double the annual S&P return, an unlikely feat. Like in the famous fable 'The Tortoise and the Hare', steady progress, avoiding material losses, prevails.

I have used several boxing metaphors in this book and won't spare you yet another one. Heavy-weight boxing and investing share a fundamental rule: *'Don't get hit'*. A surprise power shot, even by an overall inferior fighter, can knock you out cold. As we discussed in our chapter on snake eyes, there are some blows you can never recover from. Of course, only those who never play also never lose. I remember coming across an Internet cartoon showing several pencils, one perfectly sharpened and looking brand new while the rest were shorter, blunt and used up. The tagline read something like, 'You only look perfect if you haven't tried anything'. Making Cheap Option investments does not mean avoiding any potential for a loss. Recall our skewed distribution chart—there was a downside, but it was limited and far outweighed by the long tail of potential positive outcomes. Imagine playing a game where if you lose, your loss is limited, but if you win, you can win big.

Sooner or later, you will reap significant success. Avoid losses, and when you face them, make sure they are limited, and you can withstand the blow. Eventually, one of the opportunities in your long tail of upsides will come to life and deliver a successful outcome. *Sometimes, winning is the same as not losing.*

In both investing and life, consistency and avoiding losses are key. You may have heard the expression, 'You are only as good as your latest trade'. Reputation, built over years of good performance, can be destroyed by a single sizeable mistake. It comes down to trust. Even if your latest trades went terribly wrong due to events entirely outside your control, such short-term underperformance could sow doubt in your judgment or process of decision-making. Your best friend may forgive you an occasional disappointment, but next time, they will think twice before trusting you with something important.

Let's say you manage $1,000 and spread it across 10 investments of $100 each (quite akin to how a private equity fund would think about spreading its available capital). You lead the first investment and lose $70 out of the $100. You may get fired, or your client could pull the remaining funds, ending your career before you can demonstrate your ability to generate a whopping $400 gain on your second investment. A crystal ball in your possession may have revealed a $70 loss on each of the first two investments and a $400 gain on each of the remaining eight, rendering you, by the end, one of the top money managers in the world (turning her $1,000 into $3,260 after all 10 investments). Unfortunately, lacking a similar crystal ball, your client would rather fire you than trust that your investment genius has yet to shine. A 20 per cent loss, on the other hand, might earn you criticism, but you'd probably live to prove your skills and fight another day. A 70 per cent loss? That's a career-ending knockout.

You must also never think you're safe from the consequences of a significant loss. Imagine losing your entire investment in just one or two companies after years of success. This loss could mean the difference between generating outstanding results for your investors—and yourself—and settling for mediocre results. Consistency is critical. The key, whether in investing, sports, or life, is to treat each decision, each investment, and each shot as if your reputation hinges on it. Take Roger Federer, for example, who shared a powerful lesson in his recent graduation speech at Dartmouth College. One of tennis's greatest, Federer won nearly 80 per cent of all his matches. Yet, in those games, he prevailed by a razor-thin margin of 54 per cent of all points. In a competitive world, every point matters. Sometimes, a slight edge makes the difference between greatness and mediocrity. 'When you're playing a point, it is the most important thing in the world', Federer emphasised, underscoring the significance of perseverance and loss avoidance at every step of the way. He reminded us that success isn't just about shining when you're at your best, but especially when you're not. 'Most of the time, it's not about having a gift. It's about having grit'.

Defensive Offence in Action: Lessons from the Mat

Grit, patience and knowing when to strike—these qualities show up in more than just tennis or investing. They are the cornerstone of an unlikely teacher in my own life: Brazilian Jiu-Jitsu (BJJ). The essence of the Cheap Options approach is the defensive offence: protect your base, stay vigilant, and seize opportunities for a counterattack. This approach isn't just for investing. It's also seen in military manoeuvres, business strategies and sports—especially in martial arts like BJJ, which has gained enormous popularity in recent years. It has become one of the most effective combat systems in mixed martial arts (MMA) fighting. Even the likes of Keanu Reeves, Mel Gibson and Mark Zuckerberg tout their prowess in the sport. Drawn to BJJ's combative style, which reflected my approach to investing and everyday decision-making, I started training a few hours weekly in a local gym. It has taught me more about investing than I ever expected...

BJJ emphasises defence, focusing on grappling and ground fighting. Practitioners start each match with a defensive mindset, which is crucial for survival. Defence is the foundation: you learn to defend against attacks from various positions. While defending against an opponent's attacks, BJJ transitions seamlessly into offensive tactics. The defensive posture is designed to set up opportunities for swift counterattacks. It's the chess of martial arts. You observe your opponent's moves closely, adjust your own strategy accordingly, deflect attacks, and use defensive techniques as a springboard into a counterattack. It's not about strength but control and patience, using leverage and body weight to create positional dominance and minimise the risk of a dangerous attack while conserving energy and waiting for the right moment to strike.

Whether you're on the mat, in a market, or navigating everyday decisions, the mindset is the same: defend your position, stay composed, and wait for the asymmetric opportunity to strike. Sometimes, the best offence really does begin with a solid defence.

Stay the Course

But even the best strategy only works if you're willing to finish what you start. Defensive offence gives you the tools to survive and position yourself—but success still demands endurance and persistence. You may be 75 per cent of the way to success, and a single poor decision could send you tumbling all the way down.

Like Sisyphus, condemned by the gods to endlessly push a massive boulder up a mountain, success is often all or nothing. It doesn't matter how close you get if you stop too soon. No matter how much effort you've invested, if you don't see it through to the very end, everything comes crashing down.

Take private equity investing. Capital in long-term investments is typically locked up for years. You usually get around five years to deploy this capital by acquiring businesses, and five more years to then grow and sell them at a profit. Compensation is heavily back-end loaded, tied to a percentage of the generated profit (known as carried interest) and subject to a certain annual return hurdle. Private equity investors know well not to pop the champagne before successfully exiting all portfolio companies within an investment fund.

Or consider a violinist performing at the Royal Albert Hall, one of the world's most iconic stages. The audience is captivated, the hall's grand acoustics amplifying each perfect note. For 95 per cent of the performance, she is flawless, her bow moving with precision, her fingers dancing effortlessly across the strings. But in the final crescendo—just as the audience leans in, breathless—she falters. A single, jarring note disrupts the harmony. The audience applauds politely, but the magic is gone.

That one mistake overshadows the brilliance that preceded it. Oftentimes, in life, as in love or work, commitment must be total. You can't give 95 per cent, just as you can't show up for a relationship part-time or only play the violin with passion until the last measure. Staying the course means seeing things through and not stopping short when it matters most. Whether it's creating music, building trust, or nurturing love, the final unwavering step defines the whole journey.

A New Wheel of Fortune

As a distressed debt investor, the Cheap Options mindset was so ingrained in my investment approach that I made applicants' relative risk-reward preference an important part of my interview process when hiring junior team members. One interview question I frequently posed was:

'You have two potential investments. Investment A offers a chance to quadruple your money if things go well, but you can lose 70 per cent if they don't. Investment B doubles your money in an upside scenario but only risks a 20 per cent loss if things go south. Both the upside and downside outcomes are equally likely. Which one would you choose'?

There wasn't a specific right or wrong answer, but the question gauged a candidate's risk appetite and natural tendency towards risk aversion. All else being equal, I preferred candidates who chose the smaller gain with the smaller loss.

Statistically savvy readers may note that investment 'A' has the higher expected return. With option 'A', a $100 investment could result in a $400 gain or $70 loss, with an equal probability, averaging out to a $165 gain. Investment 'B', on the other hand, offers a $200 gain or a $20 loss, averaging a $90 gain. If you were to flip two coins, representing these investments, with equal probability of each outcome, you would eventually, over time, come out ahead with investment 'A'. So why did I favour candidates who chose investment 'B'? Simple: survival.

In a complex world full of uncertainties, accurately predicting outcomes is extremely difficult. Even if you do, the most likely outcome may not play out. The key to being a successful investor is understanding the inherent unpredictability of outcomes under imperfect information. Only then does the focus shift away from making accurate predictions to protecting against losses, expected and unexpected risks. Making Cheap Options choices is like spinning a wheel of fortune where each slot reads either 'not lose' (or lose very little) and 'win'. Rather than making the choices with the highest return, which often involves taking the highest risk, a shrewd investor maximises long-term returns by avoiding 'tail risks', resulting in deep losses.

An Empty Treasure Chest

The real skill for Cheap Options success lies in limiting the downside, so you can stay in the game long enough to win. That's easier said than done. One of the hardest tasks is ensuring the downside is truly limited. Sometimes, existing investors run from a situation in fear and panic for a good reason and sell to a greater fool willing to step into their shoes. Whether you bought something for $100 and watched it go to zero or paid only $10 with the same outcome, you still lose 100 per cent of your money.

Value Investing: The Hunt for Cheap Options

Imagine you're walking on a remote beach just after a storm, and you spot what looks like a shipwrecked treasure chest half-buried in the sand. The salt-crusted wood is splintered, and the metal hinges are rusted, but your heart races as you picture gold coins and glittering jewels inside. Nearby, a weathered old fisherman sees you eyeing it. 'Found it myself this morning', he says, leaning on his cane. 'I haven't opened it yet. Could be something valuable in there, but I'm too old to bother. I'll sell it to you for $100'.

You remember the story of a man who bought a painting in a barn sale for $50, only to discover that it was a priceless Utrillo. Could it be your turn today? With visions of diamonds and rubies dancing in your head, you pay him the $100 and haul it home, heart pounding with anticipation as you pry it open. But inside, there's no treasure—just waterlogged papers, broken glass, and the stink of rot. In that moment, you realise the truth: even a bargain price can leave you with nothing. The allure of hidden treasure could blind you to the risk of getting stuck with a worthless dream.

A Deal I Never Talk About

Let me tell you a story I've never spoken or written about publicly.

It was a European business—one I had grown up with, in a way. Their products were in my home as a child, part of everyday life. When the opportunity to invest in this business emerged, it wasn't just a spreadsheet exercise. There was a personal connection. A sense of meaning. A chance to help bring something once great back to life.

The founder had passed away, and the company—an old-school industrial conglomerate—was inherited by one of his children. He hadn't been raised to run a business and had spent his life pursuing an entirely different path. But when the company was left to him, he stepped in—into a situation that was already dire. The business was deeply distressed when he arrived: divisions were sprawling and unfocused, some haemorrhaging money. Costs had ballooned. R&D was neglected. Competitors had moved faster. What was once a proud, respected company was now bleeding from years of underinvestment and strategic drift. The equity had been rendered worthless. He had little experience, no capital, and few options.

To my investment team and me, it was classic distressed territory. We managed to acquire a chunk of the company's senior debt at a discount. Just like Jane Smart in our earlier example, we bought in at a level that gave us downside protection: even in a worst-case scenario—if the company entered bankruptcy and divisions deteriorated further—we believed we'd recover our money. That was our margin of safety. Our cheap option.

Of course, the real goal was different. We didn't want to get our money back—we wanted to *revive* the company. Restructure the debt, invest the much-needed fresh capital, shed the divisions that couldn't be saved, and bring the core business back to its former strength. If it worked, everyone would be better off: the employees, the customers, and even the family, who would retain a smaller share of a better and more valuable company.

The problem? The owner wouldn't jump.

In restructuring, we talk about the 'burning platform'—the idea that, like someone stranded on a burning oil rig platform, doing nothing guarantees doom. Jumping into the unknown may be terrifying, but it's the only shot at survival. And we were offering a lifeline: a negotiated deal, a significant amount of fresh capital, a future. But for reasons we may never fully understand—fear, pride, and mostly misplaced advice—he chose to stay on the platform.

Instead of cutting a deal, they filed for insolvency.

That decision triggered everything the company was trying to avoid. Liquidity issues began to deepen as suppliers refused to sell on credit and instead demanded payment in cash. The owner lost even the slimmest chance of recovering any equity value as the business continued to deteriorate. None of the long-standing creditors was willing to provide new capital to stabilise the sinking ship. The company filed in a local court, overseen by a judge better known for handling divorces and with no experience in complex corporate collapses. Worse, the company and its advisors submitted the filing without even listing us as creditors—as if we didn't exist. We were unable to step in early and provide a solution.

We called. No answer. We emailed. Nothing. I had to mask my UK number to appear as a local line. When the company's advisor finally picked up, I used the thirty seconds before they hung up to go on record: we were creditors and interested in acquiring the business. We wanted to save it.

What followed was an intricate legal cat-and-mouse game of tactical manoeuvring. We tried to buy more debt to gain leverage and be recognised as a lender. Management and advisors stirred up the workers' council and unions, painting us as the villainous foreigners who would strip the company bare. I was advised not to appear in court in person—it might not be safe.

In the end, we never got the chance to fix the business. The owner scraped together enough money to buy us out at par plus the accrued interest we were owed. We exited with a strong return on our initial capital. On paper, our investment performance was excellent. But the company, still in insolvency, continued to disintegrate. And then the owner, months later, after witnessing the devastating impact insolvency had on the business, took his own life.

I still struggle with that.

Not because I believe we did anything wrong—we didn't. We acted with transparency and urgency. We fought to avoid insolvency. We tried to protect jobs, to invest, to rebuild. And the truth is: without material external investment, the company was going to fail, whether we got involved or not. But that doesn't mean it didn't leave a mark.

This was the moment I realised that distressed investing isn't just about risk and reward. It's about responsibility. Behind every cost line in a spreadsheet is someone's job, someone's home, someone's dignity. And while we can't save every business—or every life—we have to try, with clear eyes and full hearts.

Later, serving on the board of a German company we acquired, I walked through the factories, greeted the workers, shook hands, had small chats. We knew operational restructuring was necessary. But I also saw the faces behind the numbers. You understand that a 10% cost cut might mean dozens of lives upended. When you sit in your office, staring at the financial model, it's easy to move cells around. But when you have to vote for that cut, in a boardroom with other directors, it's one of the hardest decisions you'll ever make.

Those decisions stayed with me. They still do.

Cheap options matter. But *why* you use them matters more. It's not just about defending your capital or finding asymmetric payoffs. It's about what you do with the opportunity once you've created it.

I've come to believe that there is no separation between the person you are in life and the person you are at work. The principles of good investing are the principles of a good life: resilience, discipline, humility, clarity, and above all, purpose. You don't get to be one kind of person at home and another in the office. We are what we do—at work, at home, in silence, in public, in a fight, or when at peace.

This book is about investing, yes—but more than that, it's about using investment wisdom to become the kind of person who moves through life with intentionality and character. We'll explore that even more deeply in the next chapter and the latter half of the book. Because a Cheap Option isn't just a clever strategy. It's a test: *What will you do when the odds are in your favour? Who will you become when the risk is low, and the reward is high?*

The answer, I've found, is everything.

What Cheap Option opportunities do you recognise in your life that could offer significant upside with minimal risk? How can you adopt a defensive offence mindset in an important area? What steps can you take today to ensure you're ready to take advantage of future opportunities? Who will you become when you seize them?

Key Takeaways: Cheap Options are opportunities with limited downside but meaningful upside—in investing and in life. Success often lies in adopting a *defensive offence* mindset: protect first, then decisively seize the opportunities that arise. The most overlooked opportunities often hold the greatest potential if you have the patience and discipline to wait. Sometimes, winning is simply about not losing. In the end, what you choose to do with your Cheap Options reveals your values and defines your character. The principles of good investing are the principles of a good life: discipline, humility, responsibility, and purpose. We are what we do—especially when it matters most.

Chapter 8
Cheap Options in Life

What if the smartest risks in life didn't feel risky at all?

The best decisions often look unremarkable in the moment—until they unlock massive upside with limited downside. That's the power of Cheap Options. And life is full of them—if you know how to look. Let's move beyond markets and into the real world: careers, relationships, everyday choices. This is where the Cheap Options mindset becomes your personal edge.

The Cheap Options principles that guide smart investing can also optimise the choices we make every day. While true 'cheap option' investment opportunities are somewhat rare in financial markets—investors quickly catch on, driving up prices and reducing the appeal—the complexities of life present us with abundant opportunities to find and seize these valuable options.

The approach isn't just a financial strategy; it's a natural one. Evolution itself is a master class in cheap options. Species don't undergo dramatic changes all at once, suddenly altering the entire group. That would be disastrous, risking the annihilation of the whole species if those changes were harmful or rendered the entire group unfit for its environment. Imagine everyone in Europe, for example, in the 15th and 16th centuries, looking to get to shore, jumps on a boat and tries to circumvent the world or venture onto unknown lands, both extremely risky affairs. Most of the continent would likely be wiped out. As we will see later, society needs daredevils, but if everyone out there is one, society may not hold up for long.

Instead, nature experiments on the fringes, with limited downside, if the individual members of the group prove to be unfit and die off. Meanwhile, there are massive advantages over time for the entire species, if changes prove advantageous and slowly become a dominant trait through breeding and survival of the fittest. Nature follows a Cheap Options approach.

Start With a Mindset

How do we use the Cheap Option framework in our daily lives? It starts with a mindset. Think of yourself as the business idea incubator at the start of the book, always scanning for opportunities with the right risk-to-reward ratio. Here's how someone might approach decision-making with a Cheap Options mindset:

> *I am not afraid to take risks, but I take calculated ones. The bigger the goal, the greater the risk I'm willing to take, but I never make choices that will hurt me irreparably if I fail. Whether I take risks or not, life will throw surprises at me. Life is unpredictable, and even the best-laid plans can fail. Sometimes, luck fails me several times, but I do not despair. Bad things happen to good people all the time. It's not my fault or God's, and it's not 'meant' to be. It just happens, and I won't let that stop me. I persevere, keep improving my skills, and stay alert for new attractive opportunities. When I have important choices to make, I will carefully analyse the situation and listen to advice, especially from those who disagree with me. I'll weigh the risks and rewards and play out different scenarios, visualising all potential outcomes I could think of. After a careful examination of available alternatives, I choose the path that offers solid upside with minimal downside. That may not be the choice with the highest potential reward—I will get to that highest reward methodically, step-by-step—but it's the one that keeps me safe on my path.*

To apply the Cheap Options framework effectively, you need to understand the possible outcomes of your decisions and their relative probabilities. Think of the probability distribution charts we discussed earlier. You don't need to assign precise probabilities to each potential outcome, but try to imagine the *range* of possibilities and the *shape* of the probability curve. Are outcomes tightly clustered around a likely result, or are they widely dispersed? Are some outcomes exceptionally good, while others disastrous? Are the tails to the left and right fat (greater probability) or extremely slim (very low probability)? Are the fat tails negative or positive? What are the impacts of the negative fat tails?

A fat tail risk which is low in impact may be fine to disregard. It will very likely rain today, but you'll spend the whole day in the office. The risk of rain is high, but its impact on you is negligible. However, beware of negative risks that are high in both probability and impact. The risk of rain becomes much more relevant and essential to your decision-making if you are planning a beach trip. Focus on probability curves skewed to the right, with meaningful upside and limited impact, even when downside risks do play out. At any cost, avoid fat tail downside risks with significant loss potential.

One of the most impactful applications of the Cheap Options strategy in my own life came when deciding whether I should return to Europe to be closer to my family. The move promised significant rewards—reconnecting with loved ones, pursuing my childhood dream of living in France (through an offer from the INSEAD School of Business), and giving myself time to test an entrepreneurial project I had in mind. But the risks were real: leaving behind my established network in the US and the uncertainty of a new venture. Applying the Cheap Options approach minimised the downside given that 1) I got accepted into INSEAD before leaving, and 2) I kept the option of returning to the US, where I had earned a spot in Wharton's Healthcare MBA program. This approach allowed me to leap confidently, knowing I had a safety net. In the end, the move turned out to be one of the best decisions of my life (starting a family in London), proving the value of having a 'cheap option' in place to manage life's big choices.

Without the Cheap Options mindset, I might have decided to simply leave my life and career in the US and move to Europe without any friends and family there or a place in the MBA program I attended in France. Such a choice would have introduced significant negative fat tail risks—outcomes with extremely negative consequences, but not at all unthinkable. It's not a stretch of the imagination to picture a scenario where I end up in a foreign place, with no social support network, no income and no relevant work experience in the new region, making it extremely hard to land an attractive job and maintain income security.

The Ultimate Cheap Option: Doing Good

So, what real-life decisions align with the Cheap Options strategy? Starting a side hustle while keeping your full-time job is a great example. The upside could be a significant income boost or the success of a new venture, while the downside is limited to the time invested (hopefully, compensated by the new skills you gain). Writing this book in my spare time, late at night, or on weekends or holidays, is another example. Others include starting a new hobby, learning to play an instrument, or investing in your health through exercise and research. And here is my favourite: doing good. Any good, to anyone. Acts of kindness and empathy are the ultimate no-risk, high-reward investment. Of course, being kind doesn't mean being a pushover. Admiration and respect will not come from your inability to hurt others. On the contrary, true strength lies in choosing kindness when you have the power to retaliate and destroy if challenged, but decide instead to create and love.

A good deed may not always be met with gratitude—people can be suspicious or simply in a bad mood—but there's no real downside to being kind, as long as you remain alert and ready to defend yourself if necessary. While you may not be treated well immediately in return, do not despair or change your attitude. Sooner or later, good begets good, and love begets love. This is predicated on a principle deeply ingrained in human society: reciprocity.

Reciprocity, a well-studied psychological phenomenon, underpins fairness and trust. If I help you, you'll likely help me in return. If I treat you fairly, you'll likely do the same. If I receive a favour, I am indebted to you and will pay you back. This is why we consider stealing so wrong, unfair, and criminal—it violates the basic rule that you must give to receive.

Even small acts of generosity, like offering a free cup of tea in a store, can trigger a powerful sense of obligation, leading to reciprocal behaviour. While the ultimate goal of selling a product may be evident behind the offer of a small 'free' gift by a salesperson, the principle of reciprocity remains at work: studies show customers are more likely to make a purchase after receiving such a gift. Conclusion: do good! There is no downside, but you will be rewarded sooner or later. That's why I always tell my kids, 'Be a Santa'. Everyone loves the old, white-bearded man smuggling presents through the chimney because we all love getting presents. These don't have to be wrapped in a box or bought with money. Kind words and smiles are presents, too. Don't be shy and pass them around. Love is one of the most precious gifts, and as I grow older, I realise that love cannot be kept. It can only be given away and shared. Like all worldly possessions, we cannot take love with us when we pass away, no matter how much we have received. *The only love that survives is the love we give.*

The Santa I know is the ultimate cheap option: a *free* option. You don't get penalised if you have been naughty—no risk of downside loss. At worst, you don't get a present. It's like having a go at Heaven without the risk of Hell. Some kids are not that lucky. In Austria, well-behaved kids eagerly await St. Nicholas on the 6th of December, while those on the 'naughty list' face Krampus the night before. Krampus, a half-man, half-goat figure (let's call him the kids' version of the devil), purportedly beats them with branches and sticks. In some extreme cases, he even eats them or takes them to Hell, a concept much closer to what we grown-ups may be used to—no free option for adults.

If we follow this simple principle and do as much good as we can, we will all live in a better place. There will be countless Santas, and no one will have to face Krampus. (Unfortunately, there is a flip side. Just as good begets good, pain and suffering can lead to more of the same—a different kind of reciprocity.) Why do I take such a detour here on the topic of good? Because I've long been fascinated by the idea of a global social network built around doing good—harnessing the power of reciprocity to demonstrate how acts of kindness can ripple across communities. I even have a half-serious name for it: *Goodle*. It's not something I'm actively pursuing, but rather one of those ideas that linger in the background, occasionally resurfacing in different forms. Whether it ever becomes more than a passing thought, I don't know. But the concept itself—how good spreads and compounds—is worth reflecting on.

Avoiding the Fat Tail Risks of Life

Now, let's flip the script. What are some of the choices you should avoid if you are applying the Cheap Options strategy to your life? However likely or unlikely, these choices pose the risk of a devastating loss, even though they might also promise near-term pleasure or potential material reward:

- o Take a large loan or borrow from friends and gamble with the proceeds.

- o Succumb to a lifestyle of hard-core partying with heavy drinking, substance abuse, and lack of sleep, which takes a toll on your health, relationships or career.

- o Work yourself into the ground consistently over long periods, which takes a toll on your health and relationships with loved ones (I am an advocate for hard work, but there is a difference whether you are 20 and single or 30–40 years old with a partner and kids who suffer when you are not around).

- o Go out with the spouse of your best friend, who you feel attracted to physically and suspect he or she likes you too, and have a few drinks at the bar.

- Take recreational drugs when a friend offers them at a club or party, knowing you could lose your job if caught or tested at work (which, while rare, does happen occasionally).

- Spend hours scrolling through your social media accounts when at home instead of being wholeheartedly with your children or partner.

- Take your family savings and invest them in a risky venture without consulting your partner in expectation of material profits.

- Have it your way every time you disagree with your partner and neglect their needs with a 'my way or the highway' type of attitude.

It's About You, Not Them

We discussed the dos and don'ts of the Cheap Options strategy. One more aspect is worth unpacking, and it holds life's key to happiness. The Cheap Options strategy is focused on absolute versus relative returns. Decisions are structured to minimise losses and maximise gains, despite what random forces are at play in life or in financial markets. In value investing, the goal is to achieve attractive absolute returns regardless of the macroeconomic cycle or the results of others. Being down 5 per cent when the market benchmark is down 15 per cent is, of course, a source of significant investment pride, requiring unique investment skills. Accumulating losses, however, is not sustainable in the long run, even if you consistently beat the benchmark, as investors may decide to take back their money and switch to an alternative strategy and benchmark or keep it in cash. While relative performance matters, focusing on absolute results is important in both investing and life.

We have all heard that happiness is relative. You may be happier driving a brand-new Toyota in your neighbourhood, admired by everyone else with older second-hand cars, than owning a Mercedes in an area where all your neighbours drive Ferraris. In the latter scenario, even though a Mercedes is presumably a higher-end car than a Toyota, you may feel negative emotions, such as envy, resentment, or low self-esteem. We are all tempted to assess our worth by stacking up against others. Comparing yourself to others can lead to dissatisfaction, even if you're doing well by objective standards. Instead, measure your success by your own growth and progress.

In a paper titled 'A Meta-Analysis of the Associations Between Social Comparisons and Well-Being', researchers Ethan Zell, Jason E. Strickhouser, and Zlatan Krizan reported finding that upward comparisons (to those better off than you) lead to lower life satisfaction. Suppose you generated a 10 per cent investment return, which would be a decent performance in any given year. Regardless, you may arguably feel like a failure if the broader market was up 20 per cent, relegating your performance to the bottom quartile. Conversely, downward comparison offers only temporary relief, but no lasting happiness. Self-comparison to your prior performance over time, focusing on personal achievement and growth, is the strategy that eventually generates higher well-being and life satisfaction. Our discussion on the power of compounding and the Six Sigma method of optimisation revealed that even small incremental improvements lead to material positive results over time. To foster greater happiness, focus on your own absolute performance, not that of others. This mindset, grounded in self-improvement and personal achievement, leads to greater happiness and life satisfaction.

However, while it's crucial to measure success by your own growth, it's equally important to understand that we don't exist in a vacuum. The world around us provides a context that can either amplify or diminish the impact of our efforts. As we strive to achieve absolute progress in our personal and financial lives, we must remain mindful of this world. Absolute improvement is powerful, but it often coexists with relative measures that help us understand where we stand within the larger landscape of opportunities.

Performance, after all, can be relative. Winning doesn't always mean being the greatest—it often means being better than the rest. It's like that joke about how you survive as a zebra in the jungle. You don't have to be the

Cheap Options in Life

fastest runner to escape the lion chasing you for a morning snack. You must only run faster than the last zebra in the dazzle. Similarly, to be a top-quartile performer in investing, you don't need to be the absolute best—you need to be better than most. We discussed the importance of focusing on absolute returns and self-improvement. It's critical in the context of minimising losses and avoiding complacency in the face of losses. It will probably make you happier to focus on your own progress over time than compare your current position to that of others. Yet, it is undeniable that in both life and investing, you will be judged against the status and achievements of others. If your fund is up 5 per cent for the year, while the market is down 10 per cent, you've done exceptionally well, even if 5 per cent doesn't feel like much. Being the biggest fish in the pond is often better than being the same fish in the ocean. This is not to say that you should lower your expectations, and a fish in a pond may dream even bigger than the one surrounded by never-ending water.

Winning builds confidence, which is critical for further success. Think of a student at a top university. They might be in the bottom half of their class, despite being in the top 1 per cent overall, but this could undermine their confidence and limit access to opportunities, possibly giving rise to feelings of inferiority and resentment. When top employers come to recruit on campus, they may only pick the top 10 per cent or 25 per cent of the class, looking to diversify their target school base. Meanwhile, a student in the top 10 per cent at a somewhat less prestigious school might feel more confident and hungrier for success, giving them an edge in the job market. Remember from our backgammon discussion: actively positioning yourself where you can win is critical, and sometimes tactical short-term concessions set us up better for long-term success.

In the context of Cheap Options, focusing on absolute returns while recognising the value of relative returns is not contradictory but rather complementary, providing a holistic framework for navigating life's decisions. Recognising how you compare to broader benchmarks can provide valuable insights, ensuring your strategies remain effective and competitive. Recognising this broader context—where we stand relative to others—can enhance our decision-making and help us identify opportunities we might otherwise miss. This is where a contrarian mindset can offer tremendous value, as we will explore in the next chapter.

Where can you find a Cheap Option in your life today—an opportunity that promises high rewards with minimal risk? This could be a career move, an investment, or even a personal project. How will you seize this chance to shape a better future? What simple acts of kindness or generosity could you extend today with the potential for a significant positive impact? When was the last time you compared yourself to others? How would your perspective and satisfaction change if you focused on your own progress instead?

Key Takeaways: Cheap Options allow you to take calculated risks that open doors to significant rewards, while safeguarding against irreparable loss. Seek these opportunities in every area of your life, where a small risk today could lead to great rewards tomorrow. Always be vigilant about choices that pose severe downside risks; focus instead on opportunities with asymmetric, favourable payoffs. Success lies in following the right steps in the right order, as structure often determines the outcome. Remember to measure your success by your own progress, not by comparisons to others, for sustained satisfaction and long-term achievement. And don't forget the ultimate 'cheap option': doing good.

Chapter 9
Contrarian Investing

Every once in a while, the smartest move is the one that makes you feel alone. That's the nature of contrarian thinking: not being different for the sake of it but because you see something others don't. It's uncomfortable. It's risky. And when done right, it can change everything.

If Cheap Options protect you from devastating losses, contrarianism gives you the courage to unlock extraordinary wins. The key is knowing when to zag—just as everyone else zigs.

In the previous chapter, we emphasised the importance of focusing on absolute returns—how measuring your progress against your past self leads to greater happiness and fulfilment. We also noted that sometimes relative returns can influence our feelings of success. Knowing how others have fared can help us appreciate or undermine our own achievements. In this chapter, we are going to explore another facet of being aware of others. This time, however, we'll focus on the value of analysing the decisions of others and doing the exact opposite.

In the world of investing, being a contrarian isn't simply about defying the crowd for the sake of it. It's about strategically positioning yourself where the risk is low, and the potential reward is high—very much in line with the Cheap Options strategy we discussed. By recognising underappreciated opportunities others overlook, you ensure that your decisions are not only independent but are backed by the same risk-to-reward calculations that protect you from severe losses.

Contrarian decision-making revolves around choices based on independent judgment, even when they go against the grain. To consistently outperform the market, you must do something different from everyone else—and get it right. A contrarian mindset is critical for both value investing and the Cheap Options approach because opportunities with limited downside are often overlooked by the majority. But being different comes with its own set of challenges. It's one thing to lose when everyone else is losing: 'pain shared is half felt'; it's another to lose after going against the crowd.

However, while there may be an unhappy downside, the upside—consistent with the Cheap Options strategy—can be immense. Being contrarian is critical to outsized success in investing and life. To achieve something spectacular, you must have the courage to do something different from everyone else and stick with your decision at the risk of being wrong in the face of adversity. But remember, doing something *different* from three-quarters of the market may put you in the top quartile of performance or the bottom one. Do not be afraid to be different. Go against the herd mentality or challenge the status quo, but be prepared and go with a firm conviction. It's not just about taking risks—it's about taking informed risks, backed by thorough analysis and preparation. This will make all the difference between ending on top or at the bottom. Showmanship and bravado, without much skill or training to back them up, may gain you popularity and even admiration but are unlikely to deliver long-lasting success.

Knowing When to Follow

What about just following the market? Investing in a broad index like the S&P in the United States has outperformed many top investment funds in recent years. When the market is rising, doing what everyone else does can be highly rewarding. As the overused metaphor goes in these situations, 'a rising tide lifts all boats'. But, to *beat* the market, whether it has done well or poorly, you have to do something different.

Let's illustrate this with a simple example. Imagine taking your kids to a local farm for a pig race. Four little pigs—Spotty, Curly, Skinny and, of

Cheap Options in Life

course, Pinky—compete, and visitors place bets on which pig will win. Most people don't know which pig is fastest, so they spread their bets evenly across all four. That's like investing in the market. If all the pigs run at an average speed, everyone wins something. But those who bet all their chips on the fastest pig win the most, and those who bet on the slowest get nothing. Some visitors put all their money on Curly, who falls behind early, showing greater interest in an apple tossed onto the track by a little girl. They lose everything and wonder why they thought Curly was the fastest pig (upon closer examination, now Curly seems to be the curviest of all). Skinny turns out to be the fastest pig, and those few who bet all their chips on this little lightning bolt get the biggest prize.

Over the past two decades, betting on the overall market has been a successful strategy with only four down years and attractive average annualised returns. Betting a chip on each pig has been a fantastic approach and explains the proliferation of passive investments, where investors look to replicate a broad market portfolio index such as the S&P 500 or the FTSE 100 in the UK with minimal fees. Elite investment funds that make concentrated, differentiated bets can reap enormous rewards and attract more capital if they outperform the market. The average investment fund that strays from the market, however, ends up betting on the wrong pigs.

You may be satisfied to get what everyone else does, and there is nothing wrong with that, but remember: to beat the market, you have to be different. In the race example above, you cannot relatively outperform if you spread across all piglets. The ultimate winner, Skinny was, unsurprisingly, skinny, and the majority of people discarded him as the potential winner. Perhaps those who bet on him recognised that his size could be an advantage as his bigger and heavier opponents tire faster. So, they bet all their chips on the small guy. Early in the race, Skinny fell behind and so did his supporters—just like being a contrarian investor in the wrong market cycle. In the end, however, their instincts proved correct.

Contrarian investors' strategy is rooted in superior analysis and insight and the belief that, over time, their investment choices will pay off because the odds are in their favour. This is why contrarians must measure success by absolute performance—the real goal isn't just to beat the market in the short term but to make smart, calculated decisions that build wealth steadily over time, no matter what others do. Contrarianism, while often going against the crowd, is ultimately about securing absolute returns in the long term.

The Importance of Diversification

If you're buying up higher-yielding assets, you might assume that you'll get higher returns. But it's not that simple. Imagine you're running a credit fund with 10 investments in total, and you want to beat the high-yield corporate bond index, where the average bond yields 8 per cent. You go and buy 10 bonds, each yielding 10 per cent, and you are pretty sure you will beat the market. After all, 10 is greater than 8, right? Not necessarily. A higher return usually implies higher risk. Your portfolio is different from the market but also carries greater risk. The bonds you picked yield 10 per cent for a reason. You don't consistently generate superior returns by simply picking higher-yielding assets. You also need to manage the risk of losses.

Let's look at the math. Assume your investment horizon is one year, when all 10 bonds come due for repayment. You pay 100 cents on the dollar for the bonds at the start of the year and get 10 per cent (or 10 cents) in interest at the end. The 110 cents you get back in total at the end of the year (on each dollar invested in a bond) give you an annual return of 10 per cent. But if just one of your bonds underperforms, you get 80 cents back plus your interest, instead of 100. In this scenario, your overall return drops to 8 per cent, the same as the broader, less risky index. If the loss on that single underperforming bond is deeper or other bonds also return less than 100 cents at the end, you will be worse off than the market. In this case, *being contrarian leads to underperformance.*

This is why diversification is crucial—spreading your bets across a larger number of investments reduces the impact of any single loss. Increasing your portfolio to 20 bonds reduces the negative impact of individual losses. If 1 out of 20 bonds suffers, returning only 80 cents in the end, your portfolio will now yield 9 per cent, beating the 8 per cent average return of the overall market.

However, the more you diversify, the closer you get to the broader market, making it harder to achieve differentiated results. While diversification can reduce the risk of large losses, a contrarian approach often requires concentrated positions in opportunities others miss (as those are rarely abundant). Still, as we've seen in the Cheap Options strategy, the goal is never to expose ourselves to catastrophic risk. Contrarian investing works best when it aligns with a strategy that minimises downside risk.

While it's tempting to go all-in on a bet that seems contrarian, the key to long-term success is to find those investments with limited downside while still providing attractive upside potential. By combining contrarianism with a Cheap Options mindset, you protect yourself from worst-case scenarios, while positioning for outsized rewards. The bottom line: everything in moderation, even contrarian investing. The latter should come with a built-in safety net. In other words, go in the complete opposite direction from the market in some of your high-conviction investment decisions, but invest in some more popular funds as well. Not everything the others do is going to be wrong. As a matter of fact, the market is usually right, but it pays off handsomely to go against the grain and win—only make sure to never bet the house.

A Balanced Life

The same mix of contrarian courage balanced with moderation is required in life. Being contrarian and putting all your eggs in one basket is rarely a good idea. Imagine quitting your stable career as a surgeon to pursue a childhood dream of playing guitar in a rock band. Your loved ones gently remind you that your musical talents aren't as strong as your medical skills, but you decide to go against popular opinion. On the flip side, if you pick a different hobby each week, never investing substantial effort in any particular interest, you are unlikely to excel in any of them. We'll delve into this trade-off between breadth and depth in a later chapter. There is a balance to strike, however, and the solution is the Cheap Options approach: diversify enough to protect yourself from individual losses but maintain focus by chasing preselected opportunities, offering limited downside with outsized gains potential.

Take this book as an example. It began as a deeply personal project, written in the few spare moments life allowed me—the daily commute, late evenings or early mornings, holidays, and weekends. By day, I devote myself to the intense world of professional investing, a career that demands unwavering focus and precision. Yet, I felt a need to explore a different side of myself and a passion for writing I've kept burning for years. I also wanted to reflect on the lessons I've learned and the values I wished to pass on to my sons. Writing became my way of marrying professional fulfilment with a more spiritual, introspective pursuit.

In many ways, crafting this book was my contrarian investment—a commitment to something meaningful yet unconventional amidst the fast-paced world I inhabit. It wasn't about choosing between two paths but about balancing them, ensuring that neither was compromised. More than a book, this project became a mirror for self-reflection and a gift of guidance to my children—a legacy I hope they can carry forward, no matter where life takes them. I believe the risks of my literary endeavours are limited, while the spiritual gain for me has been immense.

Ultimately, achieving success in life—and in investing—isn't about blindly following the herd or measuring ourselves against others. It's about understanding where we stand relative to the larger world, while also focusing on our own needs and absolute progress. By combining the contrarian mindset with the Cheap Options approach, you can position yourself to seize the opportunities others overlook while minimising the risks that can derail your journey. True contrarianism isn't rebellion—it's insight. It's seeing where the crowd is wrong, understanding why, and having the conviction to act before the tide turns.

But even bold choices need balance. The smartest decisions come when you weigh your inner conviction against the broader context—when you're willing to stand apart but not be blind to the world around you. That's the sweet spot: a life strategy that's both resilient and fulfilling—anchored in personal truth but responsive to the reality you move through.

The most meaningful moves—whether in investing or in life—often begin with: *"This might sound crazy, but…"*

Be bold. Be deliberate. Be different—when it counts.

Reflect on a time when you followed the crowd and missed out on something greater. How might a contrarian choice have changed the outcome? How can you apply this mindset to a current challenge, turning conventional wisdom on its head?

Key Takeaways: The greatest rewards often lie in going against the grain. By challenging the status quo, you uncover opportunities that others miss. Don't forget to diversify your 'bets' to avoid devastating losses. In life, as in investing, daring to be different can lead to the most fulfilling successes.

Chapter 10
The Psychology of Cheap Options

One fascinating psychological experiment, the Iowa Gambling Task (IGT), sheds light on the importance of the Cheap Options strategy and why it leads to optimal outcomes. Originally designed to assess decision-making in patients with damage to the ventromedial prefrontal cortex, implicated in the processing of risk and fear, IGT illustrates how we naturally gravitate towards strategies that maximise long-term value and protect us from significant losses.

In IGT, participants are presented with four decks of cards (A, B, C, and D) and asked to choose a card from any of the decks in a series of trials (the task is stopped after a series of 100 card selections) (Bechara, Damasio, Damasio, & Anderson, 1994).[4] Many subsequent variations of the IGT experiment exist, but in the original, participants are given a $2,000 loan of play money and instructed to maximise earnings on this initial loan. Two of the four decks (A and B) are disadvantageous in the long run: they bring a higher immediate reward ($100) but also carry heavy penalties that wipe out or exceed initial gains over time. Decks C and D bring smaller immediate rewards ($50) but net a higher long-term profit overall due to considerably lower penalties.

Participants typically begin by selecting cards from all four decks, as the penalties and rewards are unknown upfront, and there is a period of learning.

---

[4] Bechara, Antoine and Antonio R. Damasio*, Hanna Damasio, Steven W. Anderson. 'Insensitivity to future consequences following damage to human prefrontal cortex'. *Cognition*, 50 (1994) 7–15.

As the experiment progresses, unless their decision-making is impaired by a psychiatric condition, substance abuse or brain damage, most participants learn to favour the advantageous choices that offer smaller, safer gains. However, the learning curve takes time, during which participants continue to choose disadvantageous cards. And even once they switch to the advantageous C and D decks, they occasionally revert to suboptimal risk-reward choices. Interestingly, participants who do well in the experiment sometimes attribute their success to 'gut feelings' or intuition, which they believe helps them avoid risky choices and guides their decisions to an optimal long-term strategy. Despite having sufficiently good net results, approximately *one-third* of healthy participants do not gain a clear conscious understanding of the risks and rewards associated with each deck.[5]

In essence, IGT participants are initially attracted to decks with higher immediate rewards. However, as they experience losses associated with these high-risk choices, they generally change their preference towards options offering smaller immediate gains and losses but higher profitability over time (IGT participants with brain damage did so significantly less than the healthy controls). They recalibrate their preferences in an adaptive learning process based on negative feedback. (Disco Inferno. I learn through suffering. The great Muhammed Ali once said: 'I don't count my sit-ups. I only start counting when it starts hurting because they're the only ones that count'.)

People who prioritise lower-risk, moderate-reward options tend to perform better in the medium to longer term than those who consistently choose high-risk options. By avoiding significant losses associated with risky choices, individuals who opt for safer alternatives are better positioned to

---

[5] Siamak Aram, Lauren Levy, Jigar B. Patel, Afrouz A. Anderson, Rachel Zaragoza, Hadis Dashtestani, Fatima A. Chowdhry, Amir Gandjbakhche, and J. Kathleen Tracy. 'The Iowa Gambling Task: A Review of the Historical Evolution, Scientific Basis, and Use in Functional Neuroimaging'. *SAGE Open*, July-September 2019: 1–12.

maintain and accumulate profits over time. While risky choices can sometimes result in high immediate rewards, they also carry the potential for significant losses over time. In contrast, choosing options with lower immediate rewards typically leads to more consistent gains and fewer losses in the long run, resulting in higher overall profitability.

Three Lessons

The IGT experiment reveals three important lessons:

First, strategies that favour long-term profits are sometimes not our initial choice. The allure of significant instant gratification is too great to resist, even when it comes with high risks and suboptimal long-term outcomes. Remember our discussion on how getting unlucky at the start and suffering material losses upfront may be devastating and difficult to recover from? This is why relying on a consistent framework, like the Cheap Options approach, is crucial to help us minimise risks, avoid painful losses, and focus on sustainable gains.

Second, understanding risks and rewards is challenging. Many participants who intuitively made the right choices did so without fully grasping the risks and rewards involved. When applying the Cheap Options framework, whether in investing or in life, try instead to visualise the probability curves we discussed earlier and consider their shape. Avoid fat tail risk that could lead to material losses and look for opportunities for outsized gains.

Third, emotions play a critical role in decision-making. People learn to avoid risky choices by paying attention to emotional feedback. Let's dive in a bit deeper. Not only can we naturally experience negative emotional reactions to risk, but the pain of taking a loss significantly outweighs the pleasure of an equivalent gain. This is known as loss aversion or negativity bias and has been explored in depth by psychologists Daniel Kahneman and Amos Tversky in their prospect theory.

Neuroimaging studies show that the brain reacts more intensely to losses than to equivalent gains, suggesting a fundamental biological basis for this asymmetry of perception. What's the rough ratio of gains or pleasurable experiences needed to offset losses or painful ones? About 2 or 3 to 1. You may need two or three shots of joy to offset one shot of pain and loss. Subsequent psychological research, including work by Barbara Fredrickson, suggests a 3-to-1 asymmetric positivity ratio as a tipping point between languishing and flourishing; an equal balance of negative and positive experiences is often associated with depression. In financial markets, loss aversion may negatively impact investment choices. Afraid to sell and crystalise a loss, investors hang on to losing bets for too long, hoping to ultimately recover.

This imbalance can impact not just our financial decisions but our everyday lives. The weight of past disappointments can make us more cautious or even jaded as we grow older. It's the 'baggage' we carry with us, pressing down heavier and heavier with every loss that is never offset. It's perhaps what sends relationships or marriages down a negative self-reinforcing loop under the ever-increasing weight of disappointments. They say one way to judge whether you are happy in a relationship is to take the sum of all the moments together, count all the happy ones and hope they are more than the unhappy. What if the happy ones need to be twice or three times as many as the unhappy ones? With two kids, endless chores, and demanding jobs, this becomes a challenge—but it is a challenge that is met every day by happy couples.

In summary, while we tend to adopt value-maximising strategies over time, we often start by making sub-optimal choices. As we experience the pain of loss or disappointment, we gradually recalibrate our approach. These early mistakes, however, can be devastating, making it hard to recover. When getting back on track becomes more and more difficult, we may collapse into a vicious downward spiral of disappointments. It takes two or three shots of joy at the bar of life to counter a single shot of pain. By the principle of reciprocity, your foul mood and dark thoughts beget a joyless reaction from those around you. Hopeless? No. By consistently following a disciplined approach like the Cheap Options strategy, you can minimise these setbacks and keep moving steadily toward your goals, even when life throws you unexpected challenges.

Faith and Science

The psychological underpinnings of the Cheap Options strategy help us understand why we naturally lean toward choices that minimise downside and maximise upside, emphasising the importance of making such choices from the start. This decision-making framework transcends personal belief systems. Whether you are religious, scientifically minded, or a blend of both, the Cheap Options strategy applies with equal validity and strength. Whether chance feels like a random occurrence—a roll of galactic dice—or a divine sign of providence, this approach allows us to navigate life's uncertainties in a way that minimises risks while maximising opportunities.

While chance or external help can sometimes lead to immediate success, relying on chance alone is rarely enough for long-term fulfilment. The combination of luck and proactive decision-making truly paves the way to sustainable success and growth. This is where the Cheap Options strategy becomes indispensable—by minimising downside risks, we create space for greater outcomes when luck or divine intervention does appear.

In the Bible, for instance, the story of Nehemiah exemplifies how faith and action can work hand in hand. Nehemiah seeks divine guidance to rebuild Jerusalem's walls but takes decisive, well-planned steps to ensure success. His faith informs his strategy, but his calculated actions lead to victory—a clear reflection of the Cheap Options approach. Even in the context of Paul's teaching on *faith alone* (sola fide), true faith naturally flows into and is expected to produce tangible results through action. As James 2:14–26 tells us, 'faith without works is dead', reinforcing the need to take practical steps even when guided by faith.

Similarly, Greek mythology echoes this wisdom. Heroes, like Hercules and Odysseus, may have received divine aid, but their victories hinged on their own wise choices and perseverance. The gods provided opportunities, but the heroes had to act with intelligence and courage. This blend of external help and personal effort perfectly illustrates the essence of the Cheap Options strategy—success is not just a matter of luck and conviction but also of making calculated decisions that reduce risk and increase potential reward, no matter where you believe that guidance comes from.

Whether driven by science or belief, the principle remains the same: minimising risk through smart, consistent action brings sustainable results.

Can you identify a situation where you leaned toward immediate gratification but later learned the benefits of choosing a safer, more sustainable option? In what ways do emotions, particularly the fear of loss, shape your decision-making? Consider the ratio of joy to pain in your personal and professional relationships. How can you actively work to ensure positive experiences outweigh the negative ones?

Key Takeaways: Decision-making often starts with suboptimal choices driven by the allure of immediate gratification. Loss aversion—a fundamental psychological bias—means the pain of losses often outweighs the pleasure of equivalent gains and could send us down a vicious spiral if we experience disappointment at the start. This necessitates using a structured decision-making framework, gravitating toward strategies that offer consistent long-term value through low-risk/high-return choices, like the Cheap Options approach. Success arises from combining calculated decision-making with external forces, whether chance, divine guidance, or intuition.

Chapter 11
Plan A, Plan B, and Daredevils

Cheap Options protect us from losses that could knock us out of the game entirely. These losses may be so severe that they lead to a cycle of ongoing suffering, making it hard to regain our footing. Remember, it takes two or three positive experiences to offset a negative one. You may wonder, though: if we focus so much on defence and minimising the downside, doesn't that weaken our commitment to Plan A? If we don't have full conviction in the success of our base case, aren't we doomed to fail from the start'?

It's a valid concern. Even Arnold Schwarzenegger, one of the most successful people on the planet, who has dominated several seemingly unrelated fields, from bodybuilding to movies and politics, famously proclaimed, 'I hate Plan B'. In his view, having a Plan B means having doubts, which takes effort and energy away from Plan A. And if your dream is big, wouldn't you need all your energy, time and passion invested in it?

But let's not confuse caution, based on appreciation of life's unpredictability, with doubt. A value investor who applies a Cheap Options approach doesn't start with the mentality of 'I may lose, so I'll only risk a little'. Instead, they are confident in their analysis and underlying plan. Remember, Cheap Option choices are often not obvious and involve difficult situations, sometimes avoided by others (think back to contrarian investing, for example). Value investors recognise that while they can't predict the future, they can protect themselves from the worst outcomes. In situations with multiple, often interrelated variables, even a slight deviation in one can lead to material changes in the outcome, and unlikely events do happen.

The famous *butterfly effect* allegory comes to mind. It falls within chaos theory, a branch of mathematics, which deals with complex systems with highly sensitive behaviour to small changes in conditions. A butterfly flaps its wings in Brazil and sets off a tornado in Texas. The world is complex, with countless variables that interact in unpredictable ways. Even monumental events like Brexit or the US presidential elections could be influenced by something as trivial as the weather. A 2016 research paper titled 'Weather Affects Voting Decisions', which analysed 100 years of US elections, Brexit, and the Scottish Independence votes in Great Britain, found that the effect of wind speed could account for up to 1 per cent of the final vote. This is critical in a close election. The study contends that voters exposed to higher wind speeds are more prevention-focused and more likely to support the prevention-focused option in elections. That option may be a predictable incumbent, preserving the status quo, or the low-risk choice. On the contrary, low winds may motivate voters toward change and greater risk. A bit of wind or lack thereof and puff! The future of generations to come in the United Kingdom is irretrievably altered. It's a reminder that even seemingly minor factors can have major consequences.

Go Full Throttle, But Always Wear a Seatbelt

The Cheap Options approach is about *actively managing* your decisions to protect against harmful, unforeseen events, while still pursuing your goals with full force. In other words, it's not so much about not believing in your Plan A, but about making sure your Plan A is not vulnerable to unforeseen events—recognising that there's a mischievous butterfly in Brazil waiting to set all things asunder. If you make the right decision *at the start*, you don't need to worry about the downside at every step of the way: even if things don't go as planned, you won't be wiped out and can continue pursuing your goal.

It's like putting on your seatbelt before a race—you're ready to go full throttle because you know you are protected. If you spend too much time and effort on your weaknesses, you may not have enough time to really sharpen and magnify your strengths. If you buy a company and invest most of your time and resources protecting against competitors, you'll miss the opportunity to invest in growth and generate value. It's a subtle nuance, captured by the seatbelt metaphor: Cheap Options are a *pre-emptive* framework for making choices and evaluating alternative routes. While you need to reassess your position periodically as circumstances change, once you make a choice, you must be committed to it and give it all you've got. Drive like mad if you must, but put your seatbelt on. You cannot win without taking any risks, but you may never finish the race, unless you protect yourself against a crash.

Calculated Risks, Not Reckless Dares

Why are we then so fascinated with daredevils, those who take massive risks with little regard for the consequences—contrary to what the Cheap Options strategy suggests? The brave but reckless hero, the rule-breaker and the hot-headed desperado, the outlaw pirate who faces the royal armada, against all odds—these narratives resonate deeply with us. The same reason compels us to root for the underdog and moves us when a low-ranking sports team defeats the champions. It's the victory of David over Goliath, the rags-to-riches story, the American dream! Both the daredevil and the underdog narratives celebrate the triumph and resilience of the human spirit *against all odds*. Recall our earlier discussion on bell-shaped risk distribution: both concepts emphasise right-hand side tail risk— improbable positive events, sometimes considered luck and sometimes miracles.

Don't forget, though, that people often need to take greater risks to have a chance at greater returns. For every David who defeats Goliath, there are many more who don't make it. Out of 100 battles in alternative universes, you may place your bet on the giant prevailing well more than 50 times. High rewards often come with high risks—often leading to failure and sometimes...devastation.

That's contrary to our Cheap Options strategy and its focus on avoiding catastrophic losses. Finding choices with limited risks and high potential rewards, however, is not trivial; it requires patience, careful analysis, meticulous preparation, and high conviction. Most opportunities in life balance higher returns with higher risks, unlike the more uncommon Cheap Options that combine high rewards with limited downside.

With the luxury of a large number of possible trials, taking great risks, even reckless ones against all odds, will ultimately lead to big wins, *provided* losses are not devastating. How many people died searching for 'new' lands, sailing around the world before the famous (or infamous) Columbus? How many heroes perished in the Trojan War before the wise Odysseus devised his treacherous wooden horse? How many sperm cells die before one can reach its final target and, together, create new life? Every race has a winner, and everyone else is a loser. While history can afford and survive the tragic loss of life for the sake of the ultimate victory, individual lives are far more fragile to reckless decisions against all odds. As the Cheap Options strategy teaches us, catastrophic risks must be avoided at all costs.

Risk makes life colourful, dramatic, and exciting, but it's also what makes it dangerous. A fine balance must be struck—one that dares boldly yet avoids catastrophic consequences. Sometimes, though, we don't recognise the magnitude of the risks we're taking until we're looking back from the safe shores of hindsight. Let me take you to a time when I was younger, far more daring, and blissfully unaware of just how close I might have been to disaster.

During college, I won a scholarship to explore any topic of personal interest while committing to present my research and findings in front of the school community. At the time, I'd just joined a student-led *capoeira* club on campus—a Brazilian martial art disguised as a dance—and decided to take my curiosity straight to Brazil, coinciding with the famous Carnival. With three months free before my study-abroad semester in Germany, I emailed more than a dozen capoeira clubs in Rio de Janeiro. Only one person replied: a girl who spoke English sent me a carefully curated picture of herself and promised to help me navigate the local scene. She also had a room to rent in her apartment. That was all the convincing I needed. Soon, I was on a flight to Rio de Janeiro: no credit card, one passport, a small suitcase, and all my scholarship money sewn into the inside of my jeans.

What I didn't know was that my translator lived with her boyfriend, ominously nicknamed *Esqueleto* ('Skeleton' in Portuguese). True to his name, he dabbled in some unsavoury side businesses. After a few weeks of simmering tension, *Esqueleto*, drunk and high, threw me out in the middle of the night in an unfounded jealous rage. One member of my capoeira group took pity on me, and I found myself in Vargem Grande, a dusty, poor neighbourhood of Rio with shanty infrastructure and a reputation to match. I ended up staying with him, in a moonlit attic room he rented out to me with bare brick walls and a roof that was one-third missing. It was the kind of place people feared to tread—except the people I was with, who were the ones everyone else feared. Days were filled with training, teaching capoeira to kids at local schools (it kept them off the streets and out of trouble), and collecting interviews, music, and lyrics for my project. I even used $100 of my scholarship to help my group (the group was called *Tamandua* or 'anteater' in Portuguese) record a CD with their music in a studio—an unfulfilled dream they'd had for years. Nights, however, were a blur of danger: trudging through the surrounding jungle with locals who poached caimans with a two-barrel gun or hanging out in dubious bars, which entertained daily fights amongst the customers. The madness that surrounded Carnival erupted in situations on the streets of Rio that spelt both deep excitement and peril.

Looking back, I realise how lucky I was. At the time, it didn't feel reckless, but out of 100 such trips, I'm pretty sure I wouldn't have returned from roughly half of them. That experience changed me forever. It taught me that while risk can make life unforgettable, devastating risks—the kind that leave no room for second chances—should never be part of the story.

This is the paradox of risk. It gives life flavour and meaning but must be tempered with caution. As much as I cherish that adventure, sheer luck let me walk away with only a few blood-curdling memories.

Nature is beautiful and full of possibilities, but it's also ruthless for those who are unfit, make poor choices, or get unlucky. Losers are doomed to historical oblivion, while winners are glorified. Their legend is carried across time and generations as a symbol of a higher example; those who follow can aspire to. Without the countless nameless daredevils who go against the odds and fail, there also won't be those few who succeed. This is known as survivorship bias: we focus on what we can see. We praise the winners who have survived and ignore what we cannot see—all the losers. Such bias affects our ability to correctly estimate the odds of winning. But it may be an embedded natural bias, necessary for human and social progress. For every Arnold out there, countless wannabe movie stars, bodybuilders, and nascent politicians have failed to reach fame or any recognition whatsoever. Yet, we need an Arnold to inspire us with the power of human determination and resilience. Perhaps we need folks without a Plan B to go against all the odds, while also recognising most of them will never reach their goal. All in the name of those who come out victorious.

Nothing to Lose

That doesn't mean we should never take big risks. Sometimes a win-all-or-lose-all approach is justified. It clearly paid off for superstars like Arnold Schwarzenegger or Sylvester Stallone, who both started from nothing, had a rough upbringing, and went all-in chasing their dreams. Stallone was so broke before he sold his script for *Rocky* and played the role of the now iconic boxer, that he sold his beloved dog to Jimmy Gambina for $40, only to buy it back for $15,000 and a role in the movie, once it took off. Stallone went all in and didn't give up even when countless agents first rejected him. He was drowning in poverty but didn't want to get a regular job, afraid the comfort of the average lifestyle would seduce him to settle for mediocrity and lose his hunger.

Stallone's example does not contradict the Cheap Options approach. You cannot lose much if you have nothing to lose. Following a high-risk, high-return path is not irrational if failure would leave you roughly where you already are. In early-stage venture capital investing, focused on start-ups, most investments lose money or fail to generate attractive returns. A small portion of all investments typically generate enormous returns of 5 or 10 times the initial investment (materially higher if you invest in the early stages of a company like Facebook or Google) and effectively account for the entire profit of the fund. This approach, however, requires significant diversification across a range of investments, hoping one or a few of them would be absolute home runs. High-risk bets make sense if you diversify or have nothing to lose.

Have you ever pursued a goal without a Plan B? How did it affect your commitment and approach? Would a Cheap Options strategy have changed your results? How do you strike a balance between protecting against downside risks and fully committing to your Plan A? Reflect on a high-risk decision you've made or observed. Was the outcome a result of skill, preparation, or luck? How does survivorship bias shape your perception of success stories, and how can recognising it make you a better decision-maker?

Key Takeaways: The Cheap Options strategy doesn't weaken Plan A; it fortifies it against unforeseen risks, enabling full commitment. While bold risks can deliver extraordinary rewards, they often fail. Cheap Options minimise losses while maximising upside, offering a sustainable path to success. Success stories blind us to countless failures—survivorship bias distorts our perception of risk and reward. Big risks make sense when you have little to lose or can spread your bets widely. Knowing when and how to take risks is crucial for navigating uncertainty.

Chapter 12
Trade-offs and Sacrifice: Solving Life Backwards

Building on the strategic thinking of Cheap Options and contrarian investing, we now turn to the idea of sacrifice.

Knowing how to take risks is only half the equation. The other half is knowing what you're willing to give up. Big dreams come at a cost—but not all sacrifices are created equal. The real challenge is choosing what to give up, when, and why.

Big goals often require big sacrifices, but strategic thinking can help minimise these while still achieving significant rewards. And that's where solving life backwards begins—by knowing the destination, so you can choose the right sacrifices to get there. The Cheap Options strategy ensures that you pursue dreams and goals where risks are manageable and maximise your chances for success—not smaller goals but big dreams that can be achieved. This chapter will explore how understanding the trade-offs in life's major decisions can help you stay on course to achieve your long-term objectives.

Life's finite nature means choices and trade-offs are inevitable, requiring sacrifices to prioritise certain goals over others. One thing holds true in investing and life:

To gain something tomorrow, you must sacrifice something today.

Trade-offs and Opportunity Costs

The concept of trade-offs is critical to investing. Investing itself is a form of sacrifice: you forego spending today to generate a return on your investment and spend, hopefully, even more tomorrow. Whether you are investing in a bank's savings account and receiving interest or you are buying stocks, bonds, or property, you are giving away cash and, after all, pleasure *today*. That cash could have been easily converted into a fun overseas trip, a new car, live concerts, or a luxury spa experience. For some, the extra cash deposited in a savings account for the kids' education at the start of the month might make the difference between having three or two meals a day. You can't eat interest or have much fun with it. You are giving up pleasure in exchange for hope. You are giving up what you can do or be today, in exchange for what you can do or be tomorrow.

Economics studies how people make choices under conditions of scarcity. Our potential choices are virtually infinite, while our lives are not. Our most important commodity is time, and everything is a trade-off: a minute more you spend here is less you spend there. A minute spent in the office comes at the expense of a minute that could be spent at home. Optimise for one variable and another one suffers. An opportunity you take is another one you miss.

This kind of trade-off is known as an *opportunity cost* and it is one of the biggest sacrifices we make, whatever we choose to do. An opportunity cost is the return or benefit we get from making an alternative choice. Every investment has an opportunity cost of not making a different investment that may bring us a higher return. Deciding to keep all our savings in cash, instead of investing and taking risks, often holds the highest opportunity cost because you are missing out on potential lucrative outcomes.

This is even more relevant when we make long-term commitments that are difficult or extremely painful to backtrack. Which high school we go to, which university we attend, and who we choose to marry or be our partner are all critical choices resulting in multiyear or lifelong commitments with profound implications. Deciding to go on a date with Tim instead of George and later marrying the former may make the difference between a happy and meaningful life and one full of regrets. If you decide to pursue a career in finance, you may never know what life could be like if you had committed fully to your passion for writing.

The prior chapter discussed how portfolio diversification minimises idiosyncratic risk, but too much of it makes it difficult to achieve highly differentiated results. What's at play here is opportunity cost. Investment pools are typically limited, so buying one company or market instrument implies insufficient capacity to buy another or even selling an existing investment to free up capital.

Trade-offs in Relationships: No One Is Perfect

Trade-offs are not only embedded in all the choices we make but also in us as individuals. The personal qualities required to succeed in a cutthroat, highly competitive professional environment may differ from those required to build and sustain a loving family.

Romantic relationships have their own set of trade-offs. If you are searching for a life partner who is a caring, good-looking, and witty high-income earner with a good sense of humour, you are probably still searching. We go through romantic relationships, collecting broken shards of qualities we cherished in different people, trying to find those all at once in our next lover. We believe we can have it all! No one is perfect, however. It's a menu choice of trade-offs.

After all, life is not a fairy tale. There are no knights in shining armour, no innocent princesses forever waiting to be saved in their tall towers. It's hard to keep the passion of Romeo and Juliette and preserve their perfect love after a couple of sleepless years, changing nappies more than 10 times a day. And we only put the very best moments of our holidays with our partner on Instagram.

The divorce rates speak for themselves. Close to half of the marriages in countries like the US or the UK end in divorce. I would take a leap of faith and assume that most of those couples at the time of their wedding vows loved each other. However, the sheer magnitude of the divorce rate suggests that love at the start of a relationship has little to do with its longevity. After all, it's natural that over time, people change, and therefore, the differences between them grow. Think about how you have changed in the last year. What about the past 10 years? Think about all the possible ways your personality and preferences could evolve in the next 100 years if you could stick around for that long!

The true secret to longevity in marriage, as anyone who has been married for some time knows, is accepting trade-offs. Warren Buffet once joked that the single most important quality to look for in your spouse that would result in a long, successful marriage is low expectations. I would use the term 'realistic' expectations. We often seek perfection in the other person, a reflection of an ideal we long for and have placed on a pedestal, failing to recognise that perfection does not exist in others or ourselves.

My more than 11 years of marriage (still a modest number) have taught me that a long relationship has less to do with how much you enjoy the good times together and more with how you endure the lows, negotiate and accept differences and shortcomings, compromise, and preserve shared goals and interests, despite different objective and subjective experiences over time. And no, this does not imply settling for less, enduring abuse or being with someone simply out of fear of change. The key is understanding and accepting the trade-offs and required sacrifices and being prepared and willing to make them.

Success Demands Sacrifice: Balancing What Truly Matters

We also need to accept that sustained success in *anything* requires sacrifice. You may think that working 12–16 hours in the office and understanding your company and team's organisational behaviour and culture will make you a superstar. You may be right. But equally, it would take 12–16 hours of effort, attention, understanding, and catering to your partner's or children's needs to be a superstar husband, wife, or parent.

Identifying the right choices depends on context, as we all have different motivations and goals. Staying late in the office may be justified in the context of shared family goals if it involves working on an important deal for your career, which would benefit everyone. Spending more time with your family is certainly the right thing to do in times when they need your support. I'm not here to tell you what's right or wrong but to remind you that success requires sacrifice.

The connection between success and sacrifice is even more important to emphasise today in a world where social media makes people with no prior knowledge of or experience in investing rich, famous, or both over a viral TikTok video, buying a little-known cryptocurrency, or betting on a meme stock being pumped on Reddit. If you are chasing easy money, remember that the sacrifice you make—and the respective consequences you face—may be far greater than you expect. The principle is simple: in investing, greater returns most often come with greater risks (except for 'Cheap Options' situations when the downside is limited). Conversely, playing it safe with lower risks often means settling for lower returns. In other words, there's no such thing as a 'free lunch' when it comes to trade-offs, with one possible exception: diversification, which allows you to reduce risk while preserving your potential for returns. Don't forget though: you cannot get yourself another family to make up for a mess you left behind the same way you can diversify your stock portfolio or sell a loss-making position to buy yourself a new one.

Back-Solving: Start with the Future You Want

Whatever your life choices, getting something in the future would require you to give up something today. Therefore, you must have a clear idea of what you want that imagined future to hold. In other words, before you sacrifice, you need to understand the potential reward. Then, you evaluate the risk involved in achieving that goal and back-solve into the price you want to pay.

Obtaining a coveted promotion may require spending very long hours in the office over two years. You will largely give up your social life and effectively be 'missing in action' for your friends and family. Is it worth it? It depends. How much do you enjoy your job, and how much will your compensation increase? Are you 20 or 45 years old? Who is waiting for you at home? Will your wife or husband leave you if you deprive them of attention? How long will you likely live? We can all agree that if you know you will be eaten by a shark while on a beach holiday at 47, gunning for a promotion at 45 that would take you two years to achieve is likely not the wisest choice, in hindsight.

The goal you choose determines the required sacrifice.

Whether you are making a financial investment or trying to 'solve' your life and maximise your potential, always start with the desired result in the future and backtrack to the necessary sacrifice today. You cannot solve your life forward. You can only do it backwards. After all, this is what dreams are: a picture of a future you hold dear and wish to live in. You cannot reach a dream if you do not have one.

Ever since I was a kid, I would vividly picture my future self at a specific point in time—imagining the person I longed to become, living the dreams I held dear, surrounded by the people I wished to share my life with. In my mind, that future version of me would turn and reach back, beckoning, urging me forward. It was as if he was pulling me through time, guiding me toward the life I aspired to live. When I finally reached those moments I had once imagined, I'd close my eyes and, in my mind, reach back to that young boy dreaming of the future. It felt like a wormhole through time, where my past, present, and future selves converged—conflating dreams with reality.

You start with the dream, and work backwards, drawing step-by-step the path from that dream in the future back to you today. You would need some assumption of how long you would live and the time you have to reach your dream. You cannot assume you will die tomorrow, of course. At this extreme end, giving up anything would not make sense, as you will never get the chance to reap the benefits. My advice: *assume you have a long time, but not too long.* Thinking you will make it late into your 80s or even 90s and remain in good health may lead you to postpone the sometimes difficult choices pursuing your dream may require. Assuming instead that you have time, but just enough to reach your goals, creates a sense of urgency, channels your energy, and allows you to plan your strategy carefully without taking shortcuts.

Imagine standing at the end of the line, about to lose everything you own and dream of the very next day. You turn around and look in the only direction left…backwards. What do you see? Who have you become? What did you achieve? What made you happy along the way or sad? Who is standing there next to you on your last day? What regrets do you have, and could you have done anything to avoid them? Such backward introspection from the end to today will give you clarity of vision and help you choose between the red and the blue pill as Neo did in *The Matrix*. It will crystalise your purpose and the choices and sacrifices you need to make to fulfil it.

Back-solving to a required outcome within a set time horizon is a core principle in investing. Everything is done backwards. What will you get in the end? What's the return you want to make? The greater the risks, the greater the required return, as you need to be compensated for the risks of failing. What sacrifice is justifiable today (or how much money are you willing to pay), in view of the risks involved in reaching your goal? If the risks are too high and the sacrifice too great, perhaps it's not worth it. To make the right judgment, you must understand the potential reward at the end. Otherwise, you cannot appropriately assess the investment required. Here is an example:

I want to double my initial investment in an ice cream manufacturer in five years to reflect my required return, driven by embedded risks and the profit I could make on an alternative investment. Based on my business plan and understanding of the underlying market, I believe I can sell the company for $10 million five years later. What I can afford to pay for it today, therefore, is $5 million (in a simple transaction, assuming all equity financing). I would not know how much to spend or sacrifice today without recognising the $10 million potential reward at the end and all associated risks.

What do you stand to gain, and what are the risks? How long would it take, and how long do you have? You can then decide what sacrifice is worth it. Similar to making investment decisions, there is much uncertainty in all of these factors, and the trade-offs are strictly personal. Last but not least, make your utmost effort to stay healthy no matter what sacrifice you choose and how big it is. You may fall and get up and keep chasing your dream again, but if you lose your physical or mental health, you may be forced to give up way more than your dreams.

Wherever your journey backwards takes you, back-solving from desired outcomes must be done with the Cheap Options approach to ensure no sacrifice is too great or takes you off course altogether. Remember that the Cheap Options framework optimises decision-making but cannot eliminate the sacrifice and opportunity cost of making *any* choice.

Sunk Costs: Know When to Move On

Investing also teaches us of the risks of remaining anchored to *sunk costs*. Sunk costs are those costs that have already been incurred and cannot be recovered or changed. Decisions about the attractiveness of a project should only be based on future returns and not past expenditures. Imagine you have invested $1 million in a start-up that continues to burn cash and requires additional funding to support operations. A financial decision to continue funding the project or shut it down must not factor in the $1 million already spent but only look at the project's future prospects and whether investing incremental funds makes sense. If the project continues to lose money and returns on any new capital invested are likely poor, you have to shut it down.

Trade-offs and Sacrifice: Solving Life Backwards

In everyday life, it is far more difficult to look at decisions as a dispassionate financier would. Even professional investors hang on to losing positions for far too long based on emotional attachment or regard for all the effort and money that have so far been committed, now merely a sunk cost.

Our brain doesn't help! We are never the villains in our own stories, even when we make the wrong trade-offs or fail to accept others. Our brains are set up to justify whatever choices we make, even the wrong ones. Researchers who study split-brain patients (left and right hemispheres are effectively disconnected) show that our left hemisphere, involved in reasoning and decision-making, strives to create stories that rationalise and even justify actions it does not directly perceive, to maintain a coherent self-image and reduce cognitive dissonance or the risk of damaging our self-image (as described in *The Integrated Mind* by Michael Gazzaniga and Joseph LeDoux).

There is danger in saying the past does not matter and moving on too quickly. You cannot separate from your partner each time you get into an argument and dub all your time together as a sunk cost. Discounting sunk costs should not be an excuse to give up too quickly. However, it is also key to avoiding making an ever-increasing sacrifice that will ultimately not pay off. You must stay flexible and reassess your goal and the required relative sacrifice. While not easy, it is never too late to change your course if you are certain you are going in the wrong direction.

The faster you recognise you have made a wrong choice and dare to admit it to yourself, the easier it is to get back on the right path and minimise your sunk cost. Recognising your investment thesis is wrong (or no longer holds after a change in circumstances) and selling at a 10 per cent loss is better than holding on to a position you have lost conviction in and suffering a 100 per cent loss in the end.

We discussed earlier the power of compounding and how small incremental but consistent returns over time build up to transformative positive results. The knowledge and experience that a seasoned investor accumulates, looking at thousands of individual companies through various economic cycles, cannot be replicated overnight. The same applies to a surgeon who has completed thousands of complex procedures. I am unaware of many instances of seasoned investors turning into accomplished surgeons and vice versa. The more we grow and specialise in one branch of the proverbial 'decision tree', the harder it gets to climb back down to the trunk and take a different branch. Some choices are critical as they take a long period to play out. In the context of our limited lifespan, they exact an immense opportunity cost. *Those choices, therefore, demand proportionally large goals.*

This doesn't mean that everyone can be a Warren Buffet, reach the pinnacle of their professional organisation, become an astronaut, or receive the Nobel Prize in literature. Setting and achieving smaller goals along the way to a big dream is critical for building the confidence you need to shoot for the stars. But if you are to devote 10 or 20 years of your life to any pursuit, professional or personal, make sure it is something you truly cherish that holds enough significance to withstand the natural fatigue that builds up over time with unavoidable, tedious tasks. My music professor in a college jazz class I once took used to say: 'The best job in the world is when you love doing something, and you find some fool to pay you for it'.

Dream big and commit to dreams you truly love and find meaningful.

Age has taught me a simple truth: no one gets all their dreams, and frankly, all the fun is in the chase. How many golden sunsets can you watch over your flip-flops, margarita in hand, before you begin itching to return to the concrete jungle and start dreaming again? If you have done your best along the way, sparing no passion and effort towards a meaningful goal that gives you pleasure to pursue, you can have no regrets, even if you do not ultimately reach it. After all, we can only do the best we can. Too many factors entirely outside our control determine the ultimate outcome.

The very first backgammon game I played with my elder son when he was five, he won. It was simply impossible to counter all the perfectly timed dice combinations he rolled. A good backgammon player knows that a game lost due to the luck of the dice does not reflect skill. Who knows how long we live and what dice we roll? The sacrifice is worth it, as long as the goal is high, we play the best we can and enjoy the game.

What are the big goals in your life, and what sacrifices are you truly willing to make to achieve them? How can you minimise unnecessary sacrifices while still pursuing your objectives? If you could look back from the end of your life, what decisions would you be proud of, and what regrets would you wish to avoid? Are the trade-offs you're making today aligned with the future you want to create?

Key Takeaways: Significant goals often require sacrifices, but strategic thinking can help minimise unnecessary costs. Life is a series of trade-offs—evaluate them regularly to stay aligned with your long-term vision. Back-solve your life: start with the future you want and work backwards to determine the steps and sacrifices required. Success isn't about avoiding risk but ensuring the rewards are worth the sacrifices you choose to make.

Chapter 13
Candy Crushing and Hidden Sacrifices

While sizing up our sacrifice proportionally to our goal is key, our brains can easily be fooled into accepting grossly unattractive sacrifice-reward combinations through addiction to short-term satisfaction. Have you recently checked your smartphone screen time? How much of your day is robbed away by mindless swiping away at cat videos or admiring self-obsessed narcissists, living from one picture-perfect selfie to another? From the very start, this book tried to deliver one important message: our time is limited and precious. In whatever time we have left, chance plays a crucial role, and some of the most important events in our lives fall outside our control. We need a system to optimise our decision-making and claim back control of desired outcomes.

Our attention is constantly stolen away by relentless social media bombardment, each commercial, post or 'like', chipping away a small piece of time, but together, building up to a large black hole where time irretrievably sinks. The Business of Apps website reports that the *Candy Crush* game enjoyed 272 million users globally in 2019, it was downloaded cumulatively close to 3.5 billion times between 2013 and 2022, and users have cumulatively spent 73 billion hours on the *Candy Crush Saga* platform. 73 billion! That's more than 8 million years. What a colossal sacrifice! Imagine the sheer scale of human potential that has been invested in making same-colour bonbons disappear on a smartphone. Now imagine what human ingenuity and creativity can achieve in eight million years if the power was directed towards the field of science or eradicating global poverty and inequality—in other words, towards Good.

I remember seeing a photo exhibition called 'Removed' by American photographer Eric Pickersgill, in which he photoshopped away the smartphones and other digital devices from his portraits of everyday life. The exhibit shook me with its profound portrayal of loss. Loss of closeness, interaction, connection. There they were: friends gathered around a barbecue, lovers lying next to each other in bed, families with children sitting together at the table, and a couple that had just been married. Each of them looked away from the other in silence, staring at their empty hands. They were all together and yet all alone. Pickersgill was inspired by a family sitting beside him in a café in Troy, New York. 'Not much talking', he writes in his notes. 'Father and his daughters have their phones out. Mom doesn't have one or chooses to leave it put away. She stares out the window, sad and alone in the company of her closest family. Dad looks up every so often to announce some obscure piece of info he found online'.

I am not claiming that social media combined with smartphone technology is entirely detrimental. They allow for human connectivity and cooperation on a never-before-seen scale. AI-based large language model technologies, widely available today, could help you outline complex game theory scenarios with multiple 'what-if' outcomes, assigning a relative probability to each. While preserving agency over the ultimate decision, we benefit from a deeper and more nuanced understanding of probable scenarios. We are better equipped to identify fat-tail risks, assess probability vs. impact, and uncover hidden cheap options. Recently, I even came across a curious innovation backed by leading institutions like MIT's Media Lab—*Future You*, an AI-driven tool designed to align present choices with long-term goals. By generating an interactive, older version of the user—typically in their 60s or beyond—it claims to foster a powerful emotional connection to one's future self. This connection, rooted in behavioural science, is believed to enhance motivation and encourage better financial, health, and lifestyle decisions. Users can preload personal data, allowing the AI to simulate realistic future scenarios, where their older self offers tailored advice. Whether for financial planning, career advancement, or self-improvement, *Future You* presents a unique way to visualise the road ahead by back-solving your life from an *imaginary* older self. Indeed, the positive impact scientific advancement could have on our lives is undeniable. It's somewhat similar to nuclear fusion: the technology could be used to power the world or destroy it.

It's not the technology itself that is good or bad, but how we decide or are allowed to use it. I have social media accounts, though I commit the utmost effort to limit unsolicited content and prevent leakage of personal data. And I do play video games from time to time. If crushing candy helps relieve your stress, then crush away but keep track of time. To be clear, I do not find a veiled evil intent behind the occasional funny cat video either (as a cat person myself, I admit to having seen a few of those). The issue is that one is never enough.

Social media posts and video games create a dopamine rush, generating an irresistible urge to stay engaged. The unpredictability of rewards (likes or positive commentary) acts on us, much like in Skinner's rat experiment, leading to strong habit formation and addiction. We are no longer led by our rational decision-making but by an algorithm focused on capturing as much of your time, attention, and money as possible. Leaning on research exploring the predictive power of algorithms, the 2020 documentary, *The Social Dilemma,* suggests that social media engines can predict user preferences, behaviours, and emotions more accurately than even close friends or spouses.[6] How is that different from speaking to a car salesman focused on selling you anything on four wheels? They are pretty similar, except you don't have the car salesman knocking on your bedroom door every five minutes, aware of your deepest motivations and desires, slipping letters underneath the moment you stop responding. Our time is precious,

---

[6] Michal Kosinski, David Stillwell, and Thore Graepel. 'Private Traits and Attributes are Predictable from Digital Records of Human Behaviour'. *PNAS* 110, no. 15 (March 11, 2013).

and today's technology can thoroughly monopolise it if left unchecked, so always think of the sacrifice you are making.

As we've seen, the Cheap Options strategy, contrarian thinking, and the understanding of sacrifice are powerful tools for navigating uncertainty and making strategic decisions in life. But these tools are part of a larger picture. In the next section, we'll explore how these principles fit into the broader cycles of life and the importance of long-term thinking.

How much time do you spend daily on activities, such as excessive social media or gaming, that don't align with your long-term goals or values? What sacrifices are you unknowingly making? What strategies can you implement to reclaim and direct your attention towards more meaningful pursuits? How can you use technology to enhance your productivity and decision-making instead of allowing it to monopolise your time?

Key Takeaways: Time is precious—and often hijacked by distractions like social media and attention-hungry smartphone apps. Technology itself is not good or bad; it's how we use it that matters. Addictive algorithms and unpredictable rewards make it easy to lose control and overspend our time. But with strategies like 'Cheap Options' and conscious trade-off evaluations, we can optimise decision-making and reclaim control.

Section 3
Embracing Life's Cycles

As we reach the final section, the focus shifts from strategy to reflection, exploring the deeper aspects of what it means to live a fulfilled life. Instead of marking my middle-age milestone by purchasing a flashy sports car, a symbol of speed and escape, I found myself drawn towards a different kind of journey: one that involved delving deeper into the spiritual aspects of life alongside the practicalities of investing. This surprising detour wasn't about renouncing worldly possessions but a deeper inquiry into how our values shape our decisions in life and investing.

In this section, we examine the unavoidable aspects of suffering and the cyclical nature of life. Much like sacrifice, suffering is a constant in personal growth and investing. It's not just an obstacle but a catalyst for resilience and strength. By embracing suffering and learning from it, we can transform pain into a powerful tool for personal and professional development.

Exploring the concept of cycles, we recognise that life, much like markets, moves in patterns of ups and downs. Understanding these cycles allows us to anticipate change and adapt our strategies accordingly, ensuring we can navigate through both the highs and lows with grace and wisdom. The journey through life doesn't follow a predictable path. It's not a highway where we can speed straight to our destination without obstacles. Instead, it's a winding road, and in its unexpected twists and turns, we find our greatest opportunities for growth. By embracing this dynamic, we adapt to life's unpredictability and learn to shape it, actively managing our course with the wisdom that our choices today forge the path to our future selves.

The epilogue ties together these reflections, offering a final perspective on living a life without regrets—a life where each decision is made with purpose, and each challenge is seen as an opportunity to grow and learn.

As you close this book, take with you the lessons learned and the strategies discussed. Life is a series of investments—of time, effort, and emotion. By applying the principles of strategic decision-making, embracing the inevitability of suffering, and understanding the cycles of life, you can chart a course that leads to fulfilment, resilience, and, ultimately, a life worth *reliving*.

Chapter 14
The Value of Suffering

Suffering, much like sacrifice, is an unavoidable part of life. But, as we'll explore, it's also an essential ingredient for growth and resilience, both in investing and in personal development.

We have discussed throughout this book the importance of hard work and the sacrifice of immediate joy and pleasure in changing your odds and maximising the probability of success. In Chapter 12, we looked at sacrifice through the lens of trade-offs: for example, if you decide to take one action, you are sacrificing the opportunity to take another.

In this chapter, we explore sacrifice in the context of giving up something valuable, enduring hardship, or suffering for a greater purpose.

The Universality of Sacrifice

The concept of sacrifice is fundamental to human civilisation. It plays a central role in mythological creation stories from around the world as well as ancient and contemporary value systems: the Lord's command of Abraham to sacrifice his son Isaac; the sacrifice of Jesus for the salvation of humanity; the sacrifice of Purusha, the primordial cosmic man in Hindu scriptures, to create the world itself; the sacrifice and resurrection of Tammuz, son of a Mesopotamian goddess; the sacrifice of Iphigenia by her father Agamemnon to appease the goddess Artemis and ensure safe passage of the Greek fleet to Troy; Budda offering his own body to feed a starving tigress and her cubs. In the Maya creation story, the Hero Twins sacrifice themselves after their victory over the lords of the Underworld. They are later resurrected, maintaining the cycle of life and death. This leads to the creation of humans from maise, a sacred crop to the Maya (after unsuccessful attempts with mud and wood—different deities clearly have a different choice of material), so they could continue to honour the gods and sustain the cosmic balance, perpetuating the Twin's legacy of ever-repeating achievement and sacrifice.

There must be something universal and deeply embedded in what it means to be human that imbues the act of sacrifice. I think the latter is inextricably linked to the concept of reciprocity, which we touched on earlier, as a building block of societal norms. I get when I give. If I receive, I must give back. To succeed and receive, I must sacrifice and give. Then, as I succeed, I must sacrifice the self again in service of others so they can succeed and reach even farther through my example and wisdom.

In Maya mythology, there is a sacred bond between achievement, sacrifice, and suffering. Across various religions, sacrificial rituals involve enduring discomfort or loss, or relinquishing something of value to appease the gods and win their favour to ultimately reach success. Throughout ancient mythos and folklore, suffering is necessary for sacrifice, symbolising dedication, commitment, and a sense of moral purification. Suffering for a higher purpose. Suffering today to become who we dream to be tomorrow.

Suffering in Investing

Loss, the financial reflection of suffering, is an inseparable part of investing. Imagine the sting of seeing your hard-earned savings shrink in a market crash. Yet, within that pain lies a seed—a chance to rethink, recalibrate, and emerge stronger. Of course, the goal is to minimise suffering and avoid deep losses, but even the Cheap Options approach cannot offer painless gain. You cannot be an investor and not be prepared to suffer losses. The only way to not experience loss is to not invest at all (even then, you lose the opportunity to make greater returns). The only way to not face any risk in life is to stay in bed all day. Sitting on a pile of cash the whole way through is not investing, and lying in bed for all your days is not a life.

Of course, unexpected events occur, recessions hit, and distressed situations where bargain valuations become available may become worse before they get better. Financial pain is an opportunity for an investor to recalibrate her strategy, similar to what the IGT (Iowa Gambling Task) experiment explores. Losses reveal vulnerabilities that can be addressed and offer important lessons that would augment future performance. Uninterrupted success, on the other hand, gives rise to risky behaviour, making an investor less wary of potential losses.

Pain and Suffering: Life's Teacher

We can draw relevant lessons from here regarding pain and suffering in everyday life. Of course, we look to minimise and avoid pain if possible. But we need to embrace it as a part of life. It is an inseparable part of the sacrifice required to achieve any dream. The IGT experiment showed the importance of pain in learning and recalibrating how we make choices to optimise long-term outcomes. My son had a hard time believing me that he should wear sunscreen on the beach until he had a minor sunburn and then started asking for it himself. Dissatisfaction with our current situation propels us to try to change it, thus growing and constantly improving.

Even biologically, pain and suffering play a key role in forming strong interpersonal connections, potentially contributing to greater social cohesion. Think about the friend who held your hand through heartbreak or the loved one who stayed by your side during your darkest hour. In those moments of raw vulnerability, bonds are forged, not through shared joy, but through shared struggle. It is pain that often reveals the depth of love and the strength of connection. After all, you can only understand what pain is and what pain others feel if you have experienced it yourself. This is the foundation of empathy. The hormone vasopressin gets released into the bloodstream when the body experiences pain or discomfort. Researchers show that vasopressin plays a crucial role in social behaviours, promotes bonding and social interaction, and is associated with stronger interpersonal connection and social cohesion, greater empathy, and improved communication. During tough moments, strong social connections can provide emotional support and alleviate the perception of pain.[7] Pain can bring love.

Love is never guaranteed, but heartbreak almost always is. I've felt that sting before: the quiet realisation that something beautiful has slipped through my fingers, a reminder of how fragile we are. How fragile everything is. But each heartache has taught me something essential: it sharpens our understanding of what matters, of what we truly need, and who we want to become. And over time, we see that those moments of pain were not endings, but stepping stones—each one leading us closer to the love we're meant to find and the wisdom to cherish it when it arrives.

Pain and suffering play such a critical role in our lives that they have become a measurement of meaning. We measure the strength of our love not necessarily by how much happiness it brings us, but by how much pain we would endure to keep and protect it. The love for our partner, parents, or children is most visible in moments of need when we sacrifice our comfort or endure suffering to nurture and protect the people we care for. We all know that best friends are not those that we have the most fun going out with, but those we call when we are in need of comfort, those who will sacrifice their own comfort for ours. Those who would suffer for us.

Imagine a world with no suffering. Where the love of your life leaves you, causing you no pain. Where a loved one dies, leaving no trace of sorrow. Is this the world you want to live in? The fact is that if you spend your life trying to avoid suffering at all costs, you will suffer the greatest opportunity cost of all: life itself. If you are afraid to suffer and take losses, you will not chase any dreams, however vain or altruistic they may be.

---

[7] C. Sue Carter. 'Neuroendocrine perspectives on social attachment and love'. *Psychoneuroendocrinology* 23, no. 8 (November 1998).

Suffering for the Right Reasons

While suffering is an essential part of life's journey, much of it stems not from the act of striving itself, but from chasing goals or desires that fail to align with our deeper values. Picture yourself climbing a mountain, only to reach the summit and realise it's not the view you wanted. The exhaustion, the blisters, the sacrifices—all for a goal that didn't reflect your heart's true desire. The pain is not just in the climb, but in the realisation that you've been scaling the wrong peak all along.

Eastern philosophy teaches us that life is about accepting losses. In the end, we lose everything and everyone we love and our own life, too. For that reason, we need to learn to let go and detach from our craving for worldly possessions, which bring us suffering to desire, suffering to attain, and suffering to inevitably lose. If you ever go on one of those Virgin Galactic commercial flights in outer space, you will get closer to a Tibetan monk than if you got to his monastery and touched his shoulder. Zoom out of the planet until cities dwindle to mere specs. Somewhere in there, people in cars honk at each other angrily on hair-thin highways, spend hours in tunnels underground to get to work, vie over symbols of prestige, and dedicate their entire lives to getting a large downtown mansion, which, from where you are, is just as big as the small house on the outskirts of town. It's easier to detach from all of this when you are physically so far away. I agree with the Buddhist philosophy: the desire to have more and be better than others knows no boundary. Once we get a car, we want a better one. Once we buy a house, we want a bigger one. If lucky enough to make a million, we want two, then four. The goalpost keeps shifting, and we are forever unhappy, forever suffering, chasing an ever-shifting goal. And if we are lucky to get it all, we are forced to leave it all behind.

However, the reason for suffering is not the loss of everything we have achieved and sacrificed for. Rather, it's realising that what we suffered for was not worth it in the end, that we aimed for the wrong goal all along. Sometimes, we end up solving for the wrong equation.

Embrace Suffering

When it comes to suffering, my advice is to embrace it. Use it as a source of learning and a source of meaning or even love. Don't take shortcuts, looking for painless dreams. None of them are likely to be big.

Suffering is a measurement of meaning, and we can equally imbue our pain with meaning. A sad movie portraying loss and suffering can be just as beautiful and meaningful as one celebrating the happiness and glory of life. This will make you see suffering not as something to be avoided at all costs but as part of following our dreams and back-solving life. Think about the last time you watched a movie that left you in tears. Maybe it was a story of heartbreak, sacrifice, or loss—yet you couldn't look away. As the credits rolled, you sat there, overwhelmed, but deeply moved. The pain you felt wasn't meaningless—it was beautiful. It connected you to the characters and their struggles. In the same way, our own suffering, while painful, can add richness and depth to the stories we live, making the moments of joy and triumph even more profound and remarkable.

If I lose money on a trade, it's an opportunity to learn from my mistakes and become a better investor. If a recession hits and a business loses profitability and value, it's an opportunity to make it leaner and more resilient, capitalising on return to growth in the future. If I do what some may see as chores for my children (I have become quite the master of homemade ice cream), I see it as an act of care for those I love. I recognise that some losses are too deep to fathom or even get over: the devastation of war, the loss of someone dear. I cannot profess to know how to find meaning and a lesson in those or ask you to embrace the pain. In that very moment, perhaps you would wish to have the wisdom of an enlightened Buddhist, who can see the inevitability of it all passing and just let it go. But I know that if we merely sit, introspect, and detach from the suffering of life, without craving and chasing our goals and dreams—even if those lead to pain—life on Earth will ultimately end, even if it takes the sun to run out of fuel. And ending cannot be the ultimate purpose of life. Build rockets and follow your dreams.

Reflect on a time when suffering led to significant personal growth in your life. How did that experience shape you, and how can you apply those lessons to current challenges? Are there areas in your life where fear of suffering is holding you back from pursuing meaningful goals? How can you reframe your mindset to embrace these challenges as opportunities for growth? Can you think of a time when suffering offered you a deeper meaning?

Key Takeaways: Suffering can be a catalyst for growth and resilience that comfort and ease cannot provide. Embrace it as a part of your journey and use it to fuel your personal and professional development. Just as in investing, life's losses can guide us toward wiser decisions and more profound understanding. Embracing pain and sacrifice imbues our actions with purpose, creating richer, more meaningful experiences. By choosing to suffer for the right reasons, we transform hardship into a powerful force for personal and professional advancement.

Chapter 15
Cycles: Always Make Big Circles

Sacrifice and suffering are often the engines of transformation, social or personal, marking a shift of perspective, the end of the old and the beginning of the new. In mythology and religion, they are deeply embedded in the cosmic cycle of birth, death, and rebirth. Cycles are a natural part of life and financial markets. Even when the direction of travel is positive, it is rarely a straight line. This is as valid for the world's GDP and the S&P 500 as it is for relationships, professional growth, and life itself. (If, against the odds, you do find yourself in a romance with someone where each day is better than the one before, try to live long, and please reach out to offer some advice!)

Cycles in financial markets are driven by a combination of our proclivity for linear extrapolation (things will be ever-improving or they will never get better), human emotions (greed, fear of missing out when others around us profit, or fear of losing more, following initial losses), no tangible or absolute measure of what represents a fair value for assets, and imperfect (self-) regulating mechanisms.

Chasing profits and afraid to miss out when others are making money, investors buy into a rising market, convinced the good times will keep rolling. More buyers cause prices to increase further, vindicating the 'ever higher' expectations. Eventually, prices and valuations rise materially above what fundamentals justify, fuelled by market euphoria and lofty linear extrapolations. It is politically difficult for central banks to interfere and put the brakes on the economy, risking a recession by raising interest rates too early or by too much. And once a recession starts, and financial markets turn red, it is difficult to hold on to a stock or a bond and continue to bear increasing losses when everyone around you is selling. This, in turn, exacerbates the sell-off. Valuations reach unreasonably low levels (where nothing looks cheap enough), offering investors plenty of cheap option opportunities. When the few brave ones start buying again, making attractive investments with great returns, sentiment slowly recovers, and others jump in on the ride.

It is not the purpose of this book to explore in-depth the forces that lead to the creation of boom-bust economic and financial patterns. On the investor side, the likes of Howard Marks of Oaktree, Ray Dalio of Bridgewater Associates, Warren Buffett, and George Soros have all done a way better job than I ever could, and you should read their analyses on the financial cycle for deeper insights. The key message here is that successful investing requires you to understand the fundamentals of a business and where it stands in the context of the broader cycle. How well would this business withstand a recession or capitalise on continued growth? You then need to consider this with a view to your investment horizon. In sum, markets move in cycles, and successful investors accept and work with the opportunities and risks these cycles create—just as success in life requires navigating the inevitable ups and downs we all face. Below is a list of key considerations to bear in mind when reflecting on the impact of the cycle on your investments, followed by what these observations teach us about life.

Cycles are essential and necessary. They help weed out projects with poor returns, having only come to life due to irrationally lofty expectations and mispriced risk. The availability of unreasonably cheap financing could make even unsustainable investments appear temporarily attractive. Bigger fools have lent their money chasing high-risk strategies while expecting little compensation. The role of the cycle is to uproot commercially unsound investments while preserving and attracting more capital to those that are resilient and well-positioned to benefit from the market recovery.

Your investment time horizon is critical. Remember our George Home example and the importance of staying power in business and life?

It's hard to predict when the downturn will hit and when the upturn will follow. Therefore, maintaining flexibility is critical. It ensures resilience throughout the cycle. How long do you intend to stay invested, and is your capital secured?

Imagine you buy a stock in June that looks like a fantastic bargain, though you don't know precisely when the market will catch up with your insights. By December, the stock is down 10 per cent. By June of the next year, the share price doubles. You are a rock star! Not necessarily. Focused on financial year-end to December 31st performance, your investors may have forced you to cut unprofitable investments or else pull their capital away. In hedge funds, they may be able to do that relatively quickly. You must get it right and do so rather fast. Staying power refers not only to the ability of a business to survive but also to your ability to stay invested in it through the cycle.

If you have a long-enough time horizon and bought a great business at a bargain or fair valuation, you will make a profit eventually when the good times roll back in. This requires patience and a calm, collected approach to investment decisions. One last thing. Time is actually what defines a cycle. The economy is usually slow-moving, and changes to the system take a long time to play out. If financial markets are violently swinging up and down every couple of days instead of tracing the slower-evolving economic cycle, this is volatility, not a cycle. The difference is the time from peak to trough. While short-term volatility may avail bargain buying opportunities, long-lasting volatility makes any financial planning and investing extremely challenging.

Market perception influences reality. The concept of market reflexivity, as detailed in *The Alchemy of Finance: Reading the Mind of the Market* by the famous Hungarian-American investor and philanthropist George Soros, suggests that market prices do not merely reflect the underlying economic fundamentals. Instead, they influence those fundamentals, creating a critical feedback loop between perception and reality. You may have heard of GameStop or watched the 2023 movie *Dumb Money*. It tells the story of Internet influencer and investor Keith Gill, nicknamed Roaring Kitty, who led an army of Reddit followers and triggered an unprecedented rise in the share price of struggling US video game retailer GameStop. The company capitalised on the market frenzy and has since raised approximately $3 billion in cash from new equity issuance, substantially improving its fundamental prospects, liquidity, and ability to survive and invest for growth.

Perception influencing reality is also at the core of business marketing and advertising. Jägermeister originated in the 1930s in Germany as a blend of more than 50 herbs, roots, and fruits (a family secret) and was initially marketed as a digestive aid and remedy for coughs. When Sidney Frank started importing Jägermeister into the US in the 1970s, an aggressive marketing campaign ultimately transformed the brand's image from that of an old-fashioned digestive to a mysterious liqueur, perfect for shots and partying. Focus on youth culture and celebration and sponsorship of sports events and music tours helped turn the same cough remedy-like drink into a top-selling international liquor brand. As perception changed, so did reality.

Study the cycle and learn from how a business behaves through it. No two cycles of boom or bust are the same. They differ in cause, magnitude, duration, and impact. Nevertheless, historical data on business performance through the cycle will give you valuable insights into the resilience of a business in a recession, and its ability to grow during a macro upswing. Was the company successful in reducing costs and preserving profit margins as the broader economy declined and sales took a hit? How did the management team behave in periods of stress and when they experienced macro tailwinds? Were they conservative or overly optimistic in their planning? Did the company find the silver lining in the downturn and benefit from lowered valuations to make attractive acquisitions? Did it fully take advantage of returning demand as the economy emerged from a recession? These questions and answers hold important lessons and will give you valuable insights into how the business will likely behave going forward as the cycle unfolds.

Pay attention to the peaks and troughs. How do you make money in investing? The answer is simple: as the joke goes, 'Buy low, sell high'. That's easier said than done, of course, as the timing of the market ups and downs is extremely difficult, if not impossible, to predict. Nevertheless, most money is made and lost at the market's peaks and troughs, at its most heightened emotional states of euphoria and greed on the one hand and the deepest desperation on the other. Those who can analyse the cycle, sense the 'mood' of the market, and correctly (and often intuitively) predict when markets are close to the cycle peaks and troughs stand to reap the greatest rewards. How the cycle evolves and when the next peak or trough comes is outside the control of the individual investor. However, the investor ultimately controls her investment outcomes by deciding *when* to enter and exit an investment within the cycle.

Just as economies go through cycles of growth and recession, personal development often follows a similar pattern of progress and setbacks. The real-life lessons I draw from thinking about market cycles mirror the above observations.

Cycles in life are vital and full of lessons. A 'life recession' or a string of failures could help uproot overly risky behaviour or bad habits that lead to poor choices. It's a natural part of the cycle of personal development. When we fail, we reassess and change course while preserving what is true, important and resilient. We learn, recalibrate, and optimise. The ups and downs of life, similar to investing, provide a self-regulating mechanism. Unreasonable risk-taking and sacrifices lead to failures and regrets. Conversely, moments of deep desperation when there is nothing left to lose and everything to gain create hunger and a raw drive to pursue our dreams.

We need to be able to see the silver lining in those recessionary periods and harness the power of creative destruction of old ideas and habits. When at the bottom, embrace the freedom to pursue new goals and bold ideas when old ones have failed. Much like investors weathering a market downturn, we emerge from these periods stronger and wiser. When at a peak in our lives, whether related to our personal health, productivity, and creative power, or the strength of our relationships, we should look to extract the full benefit from the strength of our position. At the same time, it's important to maintain humility, continue following the Cheap Options approach, and make well-measured risk-adjusted choices.

Neither the bad nor the good times continue forever. Whether one was fortunate in life can only be determined by looking back at the end of it. Even when you are at your peak, reflect on the ups and downs that led to it and the downs and ups that are to follow. If our lives trailed a linear progression, we would all risk turning into frogs in boiling water at one point or another. A slow and stable drift in the wrong direction would be much harder to notice, challenge, and escape from without the violent shake-up of the down-cycle.

Wisdom is the ability to think in terms of cycles instead of a straight line. An adolescent breaks up with his girlfriend and sees it as the end of love itself and the world with it. Twenty or 30 years later, he knows that even the most beautiful of loves could end, and a new one can emerge from the ashes. He has seen it happen. There is no end to love or any journey, as long as you decide to keep going. The wisdom of the cycles is beautifully captured in an ancient Persian story I have kept dear to my heart ever since first reading it years ago.

There reigned once a wise and revered king. Hungry for challenge and desire for greater wisdom, he sends out a decree throughout his kingdom, offering riches to anyone who could make him laugh and cry at the same time. Many sages come to the palace to see him, offering stories of sadness or joy, but none of them delivers one that offers both.

Cycles: Always Make Big Circles

One day, amidst the splendour of the king's court, a humble yet sagacious outlander presents the wise king with a gift: a simple ring adorned with the inscription, 'This too shall pass'. The king laughs with all his heart, and then he cries, pondering the meaning etched upon the ring. As the seasons of his life unfurl, he experiences moments of unparalleled joy as well as those of bitter sorrow. In his deepest despair, he glances upon the ring and laughs, recognising the passing nature of life's trials. Yet, when joyful days grace his kingdom, he beholds the same inscription and weeps as he understands the ephemeral nature of happiness. The king realises that, like the shifting sands in the desert winds, both tribulations and triumphs are transient. Each chapter of his life, be it joy or sorrow, will eventually yield to the passage of time.

The importance of time. Without the passage of time, the ups and downs of life are mere volatility—random fluctuations without meaning or direction. Time transforms these fluctuations into meaningful cycles, providing the necessary perspective to understand our experiences and draw valuable lessons from them. Just as an investor needs a long-term horizon to ride out market volatility and reap the rewards of a well-timed investment, we need time to let our experiences shape us, to let our pain turn into wisdom, and our successes into stepping stones for future growth.

John Lennon is credited as saying, 'In the end, everything will be okay. If it's not okay, it's not the end'. Sometimes, all we need is more time. Just like an investor with long-term capital, giving ourselves the patience to weather life's storms can lead to profound growth and unexpected opportunities.

Many years ago, I found myself standing on the summit of San Cristobal Hill in Santiago, Chile, in a moment of personal transition. I was moving from the US back to Europe, feeling both excitement and uncertainty about the future. As I admired the breathtaking view of the city below under the famous statue of the Virgin Mary, I met an elderly Dutch couple, perhaps in their 70s, who had spent decades travelling the world. Their weathered skin told stories of countless journeys.

The man, who, as he told me, was being considered for the title of Most Travelled Person in the World, shared vivid memories of visiting my hometown shortly after the Berlin Wall fell. I was speechless. He recalled with such detail eating in a downtown pastry shop I loved going to as a kid that I could almost taste my favourite childhood cake.

We spoke and walked together for two or three hours. As we talked, the couple shared their philosophy of life. Soon after their marriage, they sold all their possessions, the house and all (I didn't ask if they had children), and embraced a life of travel, navigating the ups and downs with a spirit of adventure and resilience.

Before parting ways, the man imparted a piece of his wisdom: 'No matter where you go, always make big circles'. I wondered for a long time exactly what that meant. Why did the size of the circles matter? The answer occurred to me years later: it takes more time. The two lived in full circles, embracing each experience as a part of their journey, never rushing to leave a place. They undoubtedly had, in addition to the discoveries and wonders they experienced, setbacks and frustrations, periods where they might have questioned their choices. But they understood that time was their ally, ineluctably transforming their experiences into a coherent, meaningful narrative, allowing them to grow and transform until they started their next journey with all the lessons that the prior one offered.

Peaks and troughs are important (as well as the end). The concept of the peak-end rule, explored by psychologist Daniel Kahneman, suggests that our memories of experiences are heavily influenced by their most intense moments (i.e., our emotional highs and lows, which are the psychological equivalent of our financial peaks and troughs) and their endings. This principle can be applied to both investing and personal growth. As we discussed earlier, in investing, the timing of entry and exit—catching the peaks and troughs—defines the success of an investment. Similarly, in life, the most emotionally charged moments and how an experience ends shape our memories and understanding of our life's narrative. This ultimately allows us to shape our lives. After all, as they say, life is how you remember it.

Think about a holiday where most days are average, but one spectacular day of adventure and a joyful farewell party at the end define how you remember the whole trip. Or a love story, where despite the daily routine, you found time to celebrate your love, your special moments, and your anniversaries, imbuing them with gestures of appreciation and devotion. And when it ended, if it did, it ended well, with a closure for both and mutual respect. A touching farewell from a loved one can leave a lasting impression, making the memory of the entire relationship more poignant and meaningful. *Whoever and wherever you leave, leave well.*

In investing, exiting on a high note with an attractive return makes the whole experience worthwhile, even if it were a roller-coaster ride. By focusing on peak moments of happiness and achievement and how we end things, we can frame our personal narrative positively. Celebrating successes, happy occasions, or emotional milestones while finding meaning in the low points transforms our perception of life's journey. We can zoom in and out of these seminal moments, like an investor decides when to go in and out of an investment through the cycle. We cannot control the flow of life, but we can decide which chapters we pick for the story our own life will tell.

You can influence your reality. An ever-increasing volume of literature and studies exists on our ability to profoundly change how our brains are wired, how we perceive the world, our emotions, and, ultimately, who we are. Reading through some of these books and scientific evidence has brought me so much hope that a broken heart and even mind can be healed and transformed like a broken arm. In simple terms, our reality and experiences shape who we are. By controlling our experiences and the emotions we associate with them, we can change the very structure of our brains and, hence, our personalities. We can actively mould our environment to achieve what Roaring Kitty did with GameStop or Sidney Frank with the Jägermeister brand.

Our brains are capable of changing and adapting as a result of experiences. The peak-end phenomenon we discussed earlier is one facet of this adaptability. This can include changes in the brain's physical structure, organisation, or function. A study of Black Taxi drivers in London who prepared for the Knowledge, the demanding test requiring them to memorise the complex street layout of the city (now rendered more or less irrelevant by Uber), showed they had larger hippocampi (a part of the brain involved in navigation and memory) than the general population.

In his book *The Brain That Changes Itself*, Dr. Norman Doidge introduces us to the revolutionary concept of neuroplasticity: the brain's ability to rewire itself, change its structure, and even overcome its own limitations. Every thought you think and action you take actively reshapes the physical pathways in your brain. The commonly used phrase 'neurons that fire together wire together' relates to the findings that the more we use certain neural pathways, the stronger they become. Imagine the metaphor of the sleigh and the snow that Doidge uses in the book to illustrate this process. A single thought carves a faint path in your mind, and as you repeat it, that path deepens, becoming the default route. This explains how habits—both positive and negative—are formed, some intentionally, others by chance. But here's the empowering truth: you are not bound by your current pathways. With intention, imagination, and persistence, you can form entirely new routes, erasing patterns that hold you back and creating ones that lead you to success.

Your brain is not a static machine but a living, evolving masterpiece shaped by your dreams and directed by your will. If a stimulus results in a certain emotion, the more this stimulus is triggered, and the emotion evoked, the more they get fused together. This means that the more we focus on positive thoughts and experiences, the more our brains become wired to support a positive and resilient mindset. If certain people bring you joy and make you feel loved, surround yourself with them. If something brings you down, change it and the emotion associated with it or leave it behind. We become our thoughts, we become our emotions and experiences. If we want to change our reality, we must first start by changing our own thoughts. If you want to reach an accomplishment or have a vision of who you want to be, start acting like you already are. Imagine who that new 'you' is, what he or she likes to do, how he or she feels in certain situations and start being that person.

Doidge highlights an astonishing study that bridges the gap between thought and physical reality: participants who merely imagined flexing their muscles increased their strength by 22 per cent (compared to 30 per cent in those who exercised physically). The mental rehearsal activated neural pathways so vividly that the brain treated the imagined movement as real, sending signals to the muscles to adapt. This is not science fiction—it is the physical power of thought, measured and documented. Your imagination, when wielded intentionally, can trigger the same biological responses as the action itself. By visualising your future self, practising success in your mind, or mentally rehearsing a new habit, you awaken dormant neural circuits and genetic potentials. What you think today becomes the blueprint for what your body and mind will embody tomorrow. You are not merely imagining; you are building, neuron by neuron, the person you want to become.

Doidge explains that neuroplasticity is not just limited to thought; it operates at the intersection of genes, environment, and action. The field of epigenetics shows us that our genetic potential—what is 'written' in our DNA—is not fixed. Instead, it responds to our choices, lifestyle, and even our mental focus. Genes are like dormant puzzle pieces, waiting for the right signal to be activated and brought into play. We are capable of so much more than we believe. By visualising success, engaging in focused practice, and choosing empowering thoughts, you send signals to your genes to express their full potential. Doidge reminds us that life is a combination of chance events and deliberate choices, but your brain is the tool that allows you to steer through the randomness. The sleigh and snow metaphor teaches that even if life has etched grooves of doubt or negativity into your mind, you can consciously choose a new path, building positive habits and unlocking capacities you never imagined. Your dreams are not just fantasies; they are physical catalysts for transformation, shaping your brain, your body, and your future.

In my own life, I've found that focusing on positive affirmations and surrounding myself with supportive individuals has profoundly changed my mindset and, in turn, my reality. This process is similar to how an investor's confidence in a market's recovery can spark a positive feedback loop, influencing others and eventually leading to actual improvements in market conditions. Focusing on positive experiences and reinforcing them can shape our reality and ourselves.

Embrace the full cycle. It is essential to view our lives as a whole, integrating all experiences—both good and bad—into a cohesive narrative. Whether perceived as good or bad, each event in life is part of a larger cycle and contributes to our overall journey. We draw wisdom and strength from our experiences by embracing the full cycle. An old Chinese tale of a farmer and his horse beautifully illustrates this concept.

One day, a farmer's horse runs away. 'Such bad luck', the neighbours say sympathetically. The old farmer replies, 'Maybe. Who knows'? A few days later, the horse returns, bringing with it several wild horses. 'What great luck!' the neighbours exclaim. The old farmer replies with the same. Later, his son tries to ride one of the untamed horses, gets thrown off, and breaks his leg. The neighbours come by to empathise with the farmer's bad luck, and his response is unchanged. Soon after, the army comes to the village to conscript young men for a war. Because the son is injured, he is not drafted. The neighbours congratulate the farmer on his good fortune, and he simply says, 'Maybe. Who knows'?

Cycles: Always Make Big Circles

The cycles of life are interconnected, and attempting to cut out a piece of the cycle disrupts the entire flow. Every experience, whether a high or a low, plays a crucial role in shaping who we are. This is why embracing all parts of the cycle is important, understanding that each moment and phase is a vital component of our personal evolution. We are the strongest when we can connect the dots *throughout* our lives, through the ups and the downs, when we recognise and take in the wisdom that both the peaks and the troughs bring us.

By embracing the full cycle of life, we see the bigger picture and appreciate the richness of our experiences. Just as in investing, where understanding the full market cycle is crucial, embracing the full cycle of life allows us to draw wisdom from the entire journey. Every experience, whether good or bad, is a springboard, contributing to our growth and helping us move forward with greater resilience and insight. Just as financial markets follow cycles of boom and bust, our personal lives are a series of interconnected experiences that shape who we are. Understanding and embracing these cycles allows us to navigate life's challenges with patience and wisdom. Whether in investing or life, the key is to recognise the patterns, learn from the journey, and appreciate the cyclical nature of our existence. Remember, life is not a straight line, but a series of cycles. Embrace them, learn from them, and let them guide you to a richer, more fulfilling life.

As we've seen, life moves in cycles, just like markets. Recognising these patterns allows us to steer through both the highs and lows confidently. By understanding these cycles and applying the principles of Cheap Options and sacrifice, we can better prepare ourselves for both challenges and opportunities. As we conclude, let's reflect on how these lessons equip us to live not just a successful life, but a fulfilled one.

When was the last time you felt truly at the bottom of a cycle? What lesson or strength did you gain from that experience that you couldn't have learned otherwise? If you could view your current struggles as the foundation for your next peak, how would that change the way you approach them today? What reality are you unconsciously creating for yourself by the thoughts you repeat daily, and how can you reshape that reality with intention and vision?

Key Takeaways: Life and markets follow cycles of growth and decline—understanding these patterns helps you navigate them with resilience and foresight. Challenges aren't the end of the story; they are catalysts for transformation and renewal, preparing you for your next peak. By consciously directing your thoughts and actions, you can reshape your reality and create the future you desire.

Epilogue
Life With No Regrets

Wisdom, as defined by the Oxford Learner's Dictionary, is the ability to make sensible decisions and offer sound advice based on experience and knowledge. Throughout this book, I've shared with you the wisdom I've gathered—from my childhood behind the Iron Curtain to the dreams that took flight as that barrier fell, from the glamour of Wall Street to the serenity of $5-a-day living on a motorcycle in distant lands or in a favela on the outskirts of Rio. These lessons also come from being a father and a husband and from the humbling realisation that life is often about leaving a piece of yourself behind in others.

I've been called wise a few times, but I've been called a fool far more often. Whatever mistakes or successes I've encountered, I've passed those lessons on to you.

My fascination with bell curves and statistics is more than just an academic interest: it's rooted in a deep belief in miracles. I believe that hope is always within reach and that anything is possible. Even when life seems to fit neatly into the middle of a bell curve—predictable and mundane—remember that the tails of the curve exist. Though less likely, those tails remind us that extraordinary outcomes are always possible.

In a world of probabilities, nothing is truly impossible. In countless alternative realities, hate can turn to love, enemies can become friends, fortunes can be lost and found. You don't need Heaven to make the impossible possible, but rather persistence and belief. As long as you keep searching, what is lost can be found. Even the most complex cypher can be broken if you try enough combinations. If a door closes, keep knocking, and another one will open. When it does, have the courage to step inside. As my dad often said, 'If life throws enough lemons at you, maybe you'll have enough to make lemonade'. No matter how far-fetched your dreams may seem, remember that every extraordinary achievement began with someone daring to dream it.

Each of us has the power to create and destroy worlds—the same unimaginable energy that binds the atoms of our bodies together. According to Einstein's famous equation, $E=mc^2$, the energy within an average person is equivalent to more than 100,000 nuclear bombs, like the one dropped on Hiroshima. And yet, we are mostly made of emptiness, held together by this colossal power.

Atoms, the building blocks of our world, are mostly empty space. Imagine the nucleus of an atom as a small coin in the centre of a football stadium, with the electrons as tiny specks scattered across the field. We are nothingness and everything all at once, and somewhere in that delicate balance, the miracle of life happens. Life is precious—every life, any life. Cherish it, protect it, maximise your potential, and strive to live without regret.

This is no divine miracle with fanfare; it's the simple, profound miracle of existence. I recall a moment at the dinner table with my wife and two young sons, overwhelmed by the sheer luck of being alive at that very moment. Amidst the cold, dark, nothingness of the universe, here I was, in a warm, cosy room, surrounded by those I love the most. In that moment, it hit me—maybe Heaven isn't some far-off place we reach after death. Maybe it's right here, in these fleeting, beautiful pockets of life. And Hell? Hell is going through this entire existence and never realising that.

I cannot tell you what your life's purpose is—no one can. Life unfolds through a blend of deliberate choices and the unpredictable whims of circumstance. By back-solving from our dreams, we can chart a strategic course toward our ambitions while navigating life's uncertainties. I can suggest starting from your goals and tracing your life backwards, but ultimately, it's about your dreams, shaped by your circumstances, experiences, and lessons learned. We all start the race from different positions, and the only race that truly matters is the one we run against ourselves.

No matter where you start, following the decision-making strategies in this book can help you reach your optimal potential—your own far-right corner of the Monte-Carlo bell curve. Between the emptiness and the power of creation, the present and the future, lies the opportunity to rise to a life worth reliving. Remember the butterfly that flaps its wings and causes a hurricane thousands of miles away? Each of us matters because we have that power to bring about enormous change and be a force for good, reaching the best of our lives and inspiring others to reach theirs.

We began this journey with a shared goal: to live a life worth reliving, one meticulously crafted to minimise regrets. Regrets and suffering stem not from pursuing dreams but from setting goals that lead to unacceptable trade-offs. I cannot tell you which dreams to follow, but I have shared my thoughts on what often leads to the deepest regrets.

Bronnie Ware, an Australian author and palliative caregiver, shares profound insights in her book, *The Top 5 Regrets of the Dying*, drawn from her experiences with patients in their final days. She lists their top regrets as: (1) 'I wish I'd had the courage to live a life true to myself, not the life others expected of me'. (2) 'I wish I hadn't worked so hard'. (3) 'I wish I'd had the courage to express my feelings'. (4) 'I wish I had stayed in touch with my friends'. (5) 'I wish I had let myself be happier'. These reflections are stark reminders of the opportunities we often overlook in our pursuit of a fulfilling life.

Ware's insights, drawn from deep conversations with her patients, reveal two major 'dos' in life: First, invest time with your loved ones—you never know how much time you truly have together. As Federer puts it in the graduation speech we quoted earlier, 'Even when I was in the top five, it was important to me to have a rewarding life, full of travel, culture, friendships, and especially family'. This echoes our discussions on back-solving life: cherish every moment, recognising you may have long but perhaps not long enough. Second, express your feelings and goals freely, even if they go against the grain of popular opinion. Remember, sometimes the greatest rewards come from swimming against the tide. Don't compare yourself to others; focus on continuous improvement relative to your past self. True happiness is only relative to you.

These strategies ensure an enriching life authentically lived—a life that beckons to be relived.

As this is the epilogue of this book, where the spiritual and the practical are intricately woven, I wish to share one last story with you that vividly embodies this blend, shaping my understanding of life's balance. During a routine office meeting at a former employer, transformed by the retelling of an epic endeavour, one of the firm's senior partners shared his experience of the Comrades Marathon in South Africa. His narrative captured more than the physical challenge of an 88 km race; it painted a picture of human potential unleashed. As he described his journey through stunning landscapes at sunrise and the elation of crossing the finish line, his words inspired us to 'look up and forwards towards the future and the stars', perfectly capturing the drive to exceed our limits and aspire beyond.

However, it was the humble, poignant contribution from our office manager amidst her own personal battle with leukaemia that brought a profound depth to the conversation. Wearing a scarf to cover her hair loss from chemotherapy, she genuinely congratulated him, sharing in the joy of his achievement before adding her perspective for all of us with simple elegance: 'Don't forget to stop and look at your feet'. This wasn't a correction of the prior advice but rather an enrichment. Yet, the stark contrast between the two was riveting. Here was a person at the peak of his physical and professional life, looking forward to future possibilities, and beside him, a courageous individual nearing the end of her journey, for whom the future held no promise. She passed away a few months later, her advice lingering as a reminder of life's fragile beauty.

Her advice wasn't meant to curb ambition but to remind us to embrace the present with as much passion as we pursue the future. This balance—between dreaming of what we don't yet have and cherishing every moment of what we do—is the essence of living fully. Knowing that nothing lasts forever, we're urged not only to reach for what lies beyond but also to hold dearly to what we have now, finding beauty and value in every fleeting moment of life.

As you move forward, remember that life, much like investing, is a journey filled with risks, rewards, challenges, and opportunities. By applying the principles and strategies we've explored together, you'll be better equipped to make informed, confident decisions that lead to a life of purpose and fulfilment.

Acknowledgements

This book has been a deeply personal journey, made possible by the support, guidance, and encouragement of many. I am profoundly grateful to my wife for her patience and to my sons for their endless inspiration.

My heartfelt thanks go to my editors, Chris Murray and George Verongos, whose expertise and dedication helped shape this book into its best version. I am also deeply appreciative of my friends and former colleagues Roxana, Florian, and Lucio for their unwavering support and endorsement. To my friend and fellow author, Ali Kaden—your support has meant the world.

A special thanks to Professor Antonio Fatás at INSEAD for his invaluable advice, to my INSEAD colleague Tiziano Bruno and to Melina Mercier for their generous help. I am also grateful to Stefan Markov at ZeroBS and Alicia at Izzy Works for their creative and marketing support.

To anyone whose name may have slipped my mind but whose kindness and contributions remain in my heart—please know that your support has not gone unnoticed. I will always remember and appreciate your help.

Printed in Dunstable, United Kingdom